THE ROAD TO ECONOMIC RECOVERY

The
Road to
Economic
Recovery

**Report of the Twentieth Century Fund
Task Force on International Debt**

Background Paper by Rudiger Dornbusch

 Priority Press Publications/New York/1989

The Twentieth Century Fund is a research foundation undertaking timely analyses of economic, political, and social issues. Not-for-profit and nonpartisan, the Fund was founded in 1919 and endowed by Edward A. Filene.

Library of Congress Cataloging-in-Publication Data

Dornbusch, Rudiger
  The road to economic recovery

  Bibliography: p.
  Includes index.
  1. Debts, External—Developing countries.
2. Debt relief—Developing countries. I. Twentieth
Century Fund. Task Force on International Debt.
II. Title.
HJ8899.D.67   1989   336.3'435'091724   89-40031
ISBN: 0-87078-228-2
ISBN: 0-87078-227-4 (pbk.)

Foreword

T he debt crisis has been with us for nearly eight years. Originating in August 1982—when Mexico announced that it was unable to continue its scheduled external debt service—it triggered fears of the collapse of the international financial system. In retrospect, these fears were exaggerated. True, creditors have suffered: bank earnings have fallen, and there have been casualties—for example, the collapse of Continental Illinois. But for the most part, the system has weathered the storm.

From the perspective of the debtor nations, the situation is less sanguine. Latin American economies have on average barely grown since 1981, and per capita income has fallen. Further, the fragile democracies in which so much hope was placed early in the decade are threatened by the austerity required to meet debt repayment demands. A concern with the debtor side of the equation animated much of the debate during the meetings of the Twentieth Century Fund's Task Force on International Debt, which produced this Report, and in the end that concern strongly influenced the Task Force's recommendations.

This same concern was behind the original decision of the Twentieth Century Fund's Trustees and its late director, M. J. Rossant, to commission a series of publications, of which this Task Force is the culmination, on the debt crisis. Long interested in Latin America and the complexities of its political economy, the Fund saw in the debt crisis a rare opportunity to explore political and economic issues confronting the region. In doing so it drew in large measure—although not exclusively—on Latin American scholars. Marcilio Marques Moreira

v

wrote on Brazil, Luis Rubio F. and Francisco Gil-Diaz on Mexico, Felipe Ortiz de Zevallos on Peru, and Pedro-Pablo Kuczynski, in the only book-length study, traced the crisis in all its complexity.

The Task Force, skillfully chaired by John Heimann, turned its attention to providing policymakers with a realistic assessment of what can be done in both the long and short term. While its recommendations will not "solve" the debt crisis, their implementation might well help to stanch the outflow of resources from the debtor countries, paving the way for renewed development and a firmer base on which democracy might flourish.

I am grateful to the members of the Task Force, as well as Rudiger Dornbusch the author of the background paper, for devoting so much time and concern to their assignment. Their deliberations have made for a splendid "cap" to the Fund's efforts in this area.

Marcia Bystryn, ACTING DIRECTOR
The Twentieth Century Fund
February 1989

Contents

Members of the Task Force

John Gaines Heimann, *chairman*
Vice Chairman, Merrill Lynch Capital Markets
New York

Richard N. Cooper
Maurits C. Boas Professor of
  International Economics
Harvard University

Slade Gorton
Senator from Washington

Jesus Silva Herzog
Former Secretary of Finance
  and Public Credit, Mexico

Albert O. Hirschman
Professor of Social Science
  Emeritus
Institute for Advanced Study
Princeton University

Anatole Kaletsky
New York Bureau Chief
Financial Times

R. T. McNamar
Managing Partner
Conover & McNamar, Inc.
Los Angeles

Frank Morris
Former Chairman
Federal Reserve Bank
  of Boston

Bruce A. Morrison
Congressman from
  Connecticut

Rupert Pennant-Rea
Editor, *The Economist*
London

Kurt Schiltknecht
Chairman of the Board
Bank Leu, AG
Zurich

James Tobin
Sterling Professor
  of Economics, Emeritus
Yale University

David Apgar, *observer*
Legislative Assistant to
  Senator Bill Bradley

Rudiger Dornbusch, *rapporteur*
Ford International Professor of Economics
Massachusetts Institute of Technology

REPORT OF THE
TASK FORCE

Without new initiatives, the international debt crisis will continue unchecked. It will inhibit economic growth in the debtor nations: those nations simply cannot afford to continue to divert resources needed for development to meet debt service. What is more, "debt weariness" will make creditors and debtors less and less willing to go through repeated rituals of renegotiation. The time has come for the creditor nations to meet *their* obligations—to design new policies.

"Muddling through," the official policy since 1982, was institutionalized in 1985 as the Baker Plan. The plan, formulated by then Treasury Secretary James Baker, has served well in several respects. It has given banks time to build up capital against possible write-downs; it has allowed creditors and debtors alike to gain perspective on possible solutions; and it has made the governments of the debtor countries appreciate the need for domestic reforms. Nevertheless, national debts have continued to grow faster than national incomes.* Clearly, the time has come to rethink the policy.

The long shadow cast by the debt crisis covers far more than the economies of the debtor countries. It threatens democratic institutions in debtor countries, strains North-South relations, and poses serious political risks for creditors as well as debtors. Centrist democratic governments in debtor countries are at risk if they seem to be capitulating to creditors' demands for austerity measures, however essential. Such demands play into the hands of extreme groups on both the left and the right. Moreover, the U.S. government's influence with the debtor countries is damaged by its role as debt collector.

Global trade and financial imbalances are accentuated by the debt crisis. Debtor countries run export surpluses in order to service their debts.

---

* The debt/income ratios of the countries carrying the largest debt burdens are presented in Table 1 of the Appendix to this Report.

These surpluses are the counterpart of U.S. trade deficits. Since, historically, the United States has been a net exporter to Latin America and other areas of the Third World, it is doubtful that the present U.S. deficit can be corrected unless the trade surpluses of Latin American debtors are reduced.

For all these reasons, *the Task Force gives priority to a reduction in the debtor countries' annual payments for debt service, which will bring a reduction in their trade surpluses and allow resources to be devoted instead to development.* Third World development is critical to the economic and political health of the world. Therefore, we are setting forth recommendations designed to achieve it.

Financial Drought

The Baker Plan envisaged an eventual restoration of voluntary private lending, and was designed to avoid measures that would permanently impair the credit of the debtor countries. Under the plan, debtor countries' obligations were postponed but not diminished. The countries were expected to meet them at some future time. They were extended new credit not only to pay all the interest they owed, but also, it was hoped, to obtain extra resources with which to finance development. That approach is no longer possible. In fact, creditor banks are withdrawing from exposure in Latin America—even from those countries that have serviced without interruptions both interest and principal when due. The extraordinary difficulty Colombia faced when trying to roll over a small part of the principal of its debt and the disappointing result of the Mexican debt conversion of 1987–88 show just how far away we have now drifted from voluntary lending.

Another external source of funds for development must be found. The Task Force does not believe it should be predominantly the World Bank, which is increasingly seen as providing financial support to those countries from which banks are withdrawing. It is imperative to preserve the Bank's credibility as an independent source of new development finance throughout the world. Therefore, the general capital increase (GCI) proposed for the Bank should not be used to finance service of outstanding debts. *The Task Force believes there is a role for a World Bank affiliate in a new approach to Third World debt. But that role must not include channeling taxpayer dollars to countries that use them to pay interest to banks, while shortchanging development finance.*

What Can Debtors Afford?

Debtor countries argue that adjustments must take into account debtors' *ability to pay,* while creditors assert that the issue is debtors' *willingness to pay.* Debate on these terms is not fruitful. Ability to pay certainly has political as well as economic dimensions. Linking debt-service obligations directly to concrete indicators of a nation's economic health—for example, growth rates of real income and world prices of critical commodities—may avoid counterproductive arguments about "ability to pay."

The future credit outlook of a nation affects its willingness to pay. In the Great Depression, debt defaults were made more common, as the Royal Institute concluded in 1937, by the lack of prospects for renewed lending:

> Maintenance of debt service upon the foreign capital invested in a country is affected by a number of factors. In the first place, creditors' receipts will be dependent not merely upon the ability but also the willingness of debtors to pay. Many countries have discontinued service payments on their debts even when their financial position was sufficiently sound to enable such payments to be made. Usually, defaults have taken place when the possibility of obtaining fresh supplies of capital seemed remote, and when appearances suggested that there was little to be gained—except in prestige—from the fulfillment of obligations.

Objectives and Practical Considerations

Any acceptable solution to the debt problem must take into account the many conflicting interests involved. From a public policy point of view, solutions are acceptable only if they meet the following objectives:

- They strengthen democratic institutions in debtor countries;
- They encourage early resumption of sustainable growth in debtor countries;
- They do not prejudice growth and stability in the industrialized countries;
- They are politically and economically feasible;
- They place burdens on creditors and debtors alike.

Further, in formulating solutions to the debt problem, policymakers should keep certain practical considerations in mind:

- *Solutions should be eclectic.* There is no need to concentrate on any one approach to the exclusion of others.
- *A flexible case-by-case approach is preferable to a uniform, across-the-board formula.* The basic principles of different programs may be the same, but their implementation should take into consideration the widely different trade and growth opportunities of various debtor countries.
- *Voluntary arrangements are preferable to officially mandated solutions.*
- *The regulatory frameworks in which commercial bank creditors operate may need modification.* Stretching out balance-sheet adjustments and their tax implications may reduce eventual losses to stockholders, thus enhancing their willingness and ability to collaborate in debt restructuring.
- *The debt problem cannot be the sole responsibility of the United States.* Even though U.S. interests are strongly affected by developments in the major problem debtor countries, most developing-country debt is not owed to U.S. creditors.[1] Those advanced countries with the largest current account surpluses must play important roles in solving the problem.
- *Solutions to the problem of the debt owed to official agencies should be considered simultaneously with the problem of commercial bank claims.* The vulnerabilities of commercial banks have been in the forefront of discussion. But a significant portion of the debt is owed to official agencies.[2] Accordingly, what is done to private debt will have a major impact on the ability to service public debt, and vice versa.
- *The extensive private assets held by citizens of debtor countries outside their countries should, as far as possible, be mobilized as part of the solution to the debt problem.* Creditor country governments should cooperate in efforts to tax the returns to assets held by citizens of debtor countries. However, it appears unlikely that creditor country governments will cooperate in forcing a return of flight capital. Therefore, debtor country governments may be unable to bring about a repatriation of this capital without a fundamental change in local rates of return to assets. Cooperative solutions to the debt problem

that promote increased profitability may be a necessary lever for an early, spontaneous return of flight capital.

   • *An effective means to suspend the seniority of the existing debt is necessary in order to overcome the reluctance of lenders to extend new credit for development.* Today the existing, or "old," debt mortgages the ability of debtor countries to foster growth and profitable investment.

Solutions

Unconditional, across-the-board forgiveness is an unproductive solution to the debt problem. It unfairly taxes creditors without giving any assurance of genuine economic progress in the debtor countries. But the other extreme position—insisting that all payments be made according to existing agreements—is also a poor solution. Most debtor countries cannot fully service their external debt, except at severe economic and political costs. Paying only half the interest is already straining many debtor countries' economic performance. Banks are not willing to add to their exposure by lending any new money, let alone enough for all the interest and then more. For the moment, multilateral organizations have been filling the gaps, but even that process is reaching its limits. If nothing is done, the inevitable result will be large outward transfers of real resources from the debtor countries and continued economic stagnation in those countries, imperiling their democratic institutions.

The solutions that are found must do one or more of these things:

   • Reduce debt principal and hence interest payments;
   • Provide an extended and flexible rescheduling of interest payments;
   • Provide new credits to finance development with precedence over existing loans.

Any one of these would modify the annual flows of real resources from debtors to creditors, flows that are too large and too inflexible. A solution to the debt crisis must reduce, or better, reverse, the resource transfers from debtor to industrial countries. The challenge is to do so in a manner that least damages the interests of the creditors.

Tables 2 and 3 of the Appendix to this Report provide an overview of the problem. They show how the performance of the major problem debtors has deteriorated since 1982, and the dimensions of the effort needed to restore growth to a level consistent with the more acceptable levels of the 1970s. (Note that a growth rate of 2 to 3 percent per annum for gross domestic product [GDP] is needed simply to hold per capita income constant.) The heavily indebted countries should aim at three goals: restoring a higher investment rate, more efficient resource allocation—leading to higher social payoffs per dollar of investment—and elimination of capital outflows other than debt service. To reach these goals, it will be necessary for the debtor nations to increase both their domestic saving rates and their net inflows of capital. Greater foreign resource inflows should be conditional on the implementation of measures to increase the rate of domestic saving as well as efficiency in allocation. To achieve the targets set out in Table 2, annual net capital inflows must increase by about 2.4 percent of the heavily indebted countries' GDP, or about $25 billion compared to the flows of 1987. Domestic saving must increase by approximately the same amount.

The central practical problem is to provide institutions that will make these goals possible. Such institutions can reduce the burden of debt-service outflows in two general ways. First, they can postpone current debt-service obligations through interest capitalization and recycling. This increases future obligations, but it allows time for debtors to build their capacity to meet such obligations without excessive pressure on consumption, investment, or foreign exchange earnings. Second, they can reduce the level of debt through debt-equity swaps, repurchases of debt in the secondary market, or other means.

Each of these approaches to debt service relief has problems. New lending creates greater debt-service obligations in the future; output and exports must grow robustly for the debt burden to lessen. Reduction of the debt stock is no panacea either: blanket debt relief can abort policy reform; it can capriciously and unfairly allocate costs of the mistakes that led to the debt problem; and, finally, it may not solve the problem at all. Even if a large fraction of some countries' debt disappeared, they could not service their remaining debt obligations.

The Task Force believes that a combination of several institutional arrangements is likely to be most successful. Measures that postpone payment should be combined with measures that use the secondary market for debt reduction. As postponement of obligations can be achieved more quickly than creation of new institutions to manage debt reduction, we will consider interest recycling and adjustments first and then turn to debt reduction. We will look at:

- Recycling of interest payments into new flows of capital to the debtor countries;
- Adjustment of interest payments to reflect changes in economic conditions;
- Use of market-related mechanisms to reduce debt;
- Establishment of a central international facility for debt-service reduction and management.

The Task Force believes that the prime goal of such arrangements is to reverse the flow of resources between creditor and debtor countries while keeping in place incentives to the debtors to restructure their economies and increase productive investment. Admittedly, reconstruction of debtor economies is a long-term problem. The Task Force's recommendations are aimed at keeping resource flows between developed and developing countries steady and predictable, encouraging vigorous economic growth. Only then will the debtor countries' economies be rebuilt, making debt repayable. The most important institutional innovations, in this light, are those that replace piecemeal, contentious renegotiation and rescheduling of debt with more automatic procedures to defer and capitalize interest payments and to reduce and restructure principal.

Recycling of Interest Payments

Any substantial change in the flow of resources out of debtor countries must deal with the flow of interest payments. Today debtor countries are paying, on average, half the interest they owe. Therefore, even as debt piles on top of debt—as part of the interest due is financed by new loans—the remaining interest is actually paid at the expense of domestic investment. Partial debt forgiveness alone will not solve the problem. Even a program that achieves a significant write-down of debts, say 35 percent, will not solve the immediate transfer problem if all the interest on the written-down debt must be paid on schedule. Following a renegotiation and reduction of its debt, a country like Argentina is just as likely to be unable to pay the remaining interest due as it is today.

The Task Force thus believes that the best approach is a fundamental rescheduling of debt service that substantially reduces the interest payments due in the near future. Full interest payment in dollars would be made only on trade credit. The remaining interest payments would in part be capitalized and in part be paid in local currency. The relative weight of these portions would depend on a country's ability to pay.

To the extent that interest payments are capitalized, resources are freed for much-needed public investment. Creditors who receive the local currency payments could use them for investment in the debtor countries' economies. The only limitation on the use of the funds would be that they cannot be transferred abroad for some specified period of time. The claims to these payments could, however, be sold. Basically this scheme parallels a debt-equity swap, as discussed below, but it applies to interest payments rather than to the principal. It amounts to a local currency recycling of interest payments to finance reconstruction and development.

The advantages of interest recycling are threefold. First, the transfer abroad of resources is suspended. Rather than running trade surpluses, debtor countries have imports or domestic resources to devote to investment. Of course, budget action is required to assure that in fact the resources go into investment rather than consumption. The shift of resources toward investment expands capacity and creates jobs, critical developments in economies with high unemployment and rapid labor force growth. Expansion in capacity removes bottlenecks to growth. Growth can then translate into more stable public finance via a broadened tax base.

A second important by-product would be the creation of a more stable business environment. Under the current strategy, a foreign exchange crisis is always around the corner—invariably bringing contraction of demand and exchange depreciation. The dismal outlook discourages productive domestic investment and promotes capital flight. Without the need for immediate debt service, the debtor economy can catch its breath and embark on a course of long-term investment and growth. Restoration of business confidence may also bring flight capital home.

There is also a third gain. In the present situation, the need to reduce the real exchange rate to improve the trade balance translates into inflationary pressure. Removing external constraints might allow some real appreciation, providing breathing space for stabilization of inflation, an essential step to restoring normal business conditions.

In return for their creditors' acceptance of an interest recycling scheme, debtor countries would commit themselves to adjustment programs. These reforms would diminish excessive nationalism, facilitate legislative action to attract private foreign investment, and promote serious budget reforms to free resources for public sector investment. Budget reforms would include more efficient, broader-base taxation and cuts in wasteful spending. The temptation to dissipate the resources into a restoration of consumption after so many years of deprivation will be strong, but must be resisted.

*The Task Force believes that tough-minded fiscal measures and broad-based liberalization of investment opportunities are the quid pro quo for the suspension of resource transfers. There must be no misconception: debtor countries will have to undertake major policy reforms to ensure that the leeway provided by recycling is used productively.**

Adjustment programs inevitably create political strains. Thus, although creditors and taxpayers in creditor countries have a right to expect ad-

---

* *Albert O. Hirschman dissents:*

I share broadly in the belief that debt relief would be most successful if it were preceded or followed by the kind of domestic policies in debtor countries that are advocated here. I would be in favor of holding intensive discussions between debtors and creditors on desirable policies but feel strongly that it is wrong to insist on formal agreement by debtor countries to such policies as "part of any package" on debt relief. In the first place, the imposition by creditor countries of "reforms," that is, of substantial changes in central domestic policies of the debtor countries, is highly intrusive and amounts in fact to a violation of the debtors' sovereignty. More important perhaps, such a compact is either unnecessary, when the debtor country sincerely wishes to institute such reforms, or ineffective and counterproductive, because of assured backsliding in the future, when the country pays only lip service to them. Thirdly, policy reform in the debtor countries should in no sense be regarded as a "counterpart" or "quid pro quo" the creditors get in exchange for debt relief; as pointed out elsewhere in this Report, debt relief is very much in the self-interest of the creditors because of the ensuing rise in their exports of capital goods as well as for more general economic and political reasons. Some twenty years ago, I argued along very similar lines, and in considerable detail, against "Buying Virtue through Aid" in an article, co-authored with Richard M. Bird, "Foreign Aid: A Critique and a Proposal," *Princeton Essays in International Finance,* no. 69, July 1968, reprinted in my collection *A Bias for Hope: Essays on Development and Latin America* (New Haven: Yale University Press, 1971), particularly pp. 198-210.

Jesus Silva Herzog concurs with Mr. Hirschman.

Kurt Schiltknecht also dissents:

However, I am of the opinion that one should even more strongly emphasize the fact that the basic solution of the problem has to start within the indebted countries themselves, for example, price stability, reduction of the budget deficits, free enterprise, and so forth.

justment, their stance should be cooperative, not intrusive. The reform program that accompanies interest recycling should be treated as a domestic development program. To put this in historical perspective, a domestic program of this nature, which would extend over a decade or so, could be likened to the long-term reconstruction programs for Europe that followed World War I and World War II.

The basic case for this program is that it emphasizes economic development. Since debtors today are not improving their ability to service their debts and debt is becoming politicized, the creditors' interests too are best served by a program that restores growth. Unfortunately, the current negotiation process does not lend itself to restructuring debts productively. As a result, policy intervention by the creditors (or responsible unilateral action by debtor nations) is needed to break the deadlock.

Interest Payment Adjustments

Existing debt contracts are particularly unsuited to the circumstances of borrowing countries. They set fixed debt-service schedules at rates geared to world interest rates. Thus they invite crises of illiquidity due to temporary shocks to debtors' terms of trade, transitory high interest rates in advanced countries, and losses in export demands or supplies.

The Task Force believes that countries would be in a better position to service their debts if debt-service schedules were more flexible—that is, if changes in objective indicators were used to trigger automatic deferments of portions of interest payments. This would obviously be the case for transitory disturbances. But even when adverse disturbances were not subsequently reversed, such flexibility would allow more time for essential adjustments. Of course, flexible interest payments increase the exposure of commercial banks, which would be lending for longer periods just when their borrowers are having difficulties.

Interest adjustment is most obviously desirable for those countries where a single world price, say the price of oil, has a major effect on balance of payments, real income, and public finance. But the method can also be applied in a more general fashion by using the growth rate of per capita income as the benchmark that governs debt service. Another possibility, recognizing in particular the external transfer problem, would be to use export earnings as the criterion for triggering changes in current debt-service liabilities.

Flexibility can also be used in those cases where continued debt service on contractual terms seems totally precluded—for example, Bolivia or Peru. But there should be a counterpart: in exchange for a reduction of debt service under adverse conditions, a country should agree to resume debt service when conditions improve beyond a specified threshold. Thus creditors keep the option value of any improvements in the debtor countries as a partial offset to their sacrifice of current interest earnings.

Using the Secondary Markets for Debt Instruments

Over the past few years, an active but thin secondary market for developing-country debts has emerged. In this market the debts trade at a significant discount. These discounts have elicited interest in a number of schemes that would allow investors and/or debtor countries to take advantage of this market. *Although market mechanisms offer only limited hope of debt reduction, the Task Force believes that devices such as debt-equity swaps and buy-backs merit consideration.* Let us now consider how these mechanisms work.

Debt-Equity Swaps. In a debt-equity swap, a private investor purchases debt on the secondary market and presents the claim to the debtor government for payment in local currency, which is then used for investment in the debtor country. The success of debt-equity swaps depends on a number of factors in each case. In the extreme, debt-equity swaps may merely replace a dollar money inflow that would have occurred anyway; the debtor country pays off dollar debt without sharing significantly in the discount. At the other extreme, the swap may induce new foreign investment and allow the debtor country government to reap most of the discount.

There is some illusion about the ultimate balance-of-payments effects resulting from debt-equity programs. They give rise to profit remittances down the road in return for immediate reduction in interest outflows. The net effect could be either favorable or unfavorable. Moreover, debt-equity swaps can be misused, as now appears to be happening in Brazil. At the same time as debt is swapped for cruzados, external payments in dollars are arranged illicitly, dressed up as profit remittances. A major shift in this direction may well spoil the regulatory climate for bona fide investment.

Buy-backs. In the 1930s and 1940s, the defaulted debt of Latin America traded at large discounts, and much of it was ultimately bought and "repatriated" by the debtor governments. At the time, debt holders' protective councils severely protested this practice. They argued that the dollars that could be used for interest payments should not instead be used to buy back bonds at deep discounts when these discounts reflected primarily an unwillingness to pay.

Today the *pari passu* clause in commercial bank debt contracts proscribes buy-backs, but the idea that debtor countries could achieve important debt reduction in this way is widely accepted. Several countries have in fact used the secondary market to buy back some private debts. Although repurchase of private debt has taken place on a large scale in the case of Mexico, public debts so far have apparently not been repurchased in significant amounts (except for Bolivia).

The scope for buy-backs is intrinsically limited. To be able to buy back the claims against it on a large scale, a debtor needs resources that, if available for debt service, would prevent those claims from trading at a large discount. Only when information is very imperfect, when creditors are very impatient, or when regulatory and tax considerations create asymmetries will debtors be able to retire debt advantageously. But even then the amounts will tend to be minor. The only case in which to expect large-scale buy-backs is one in which commercial banks believe, rightly or wrongly, that one piece of Latin American debt is as bad as another, whatever the debtor country. In that case, there is room for the better-placed countries to take advantage of the undiscriminating across-the-board discount.

In principle, buy-backs might be a means for repatriating private capital that has fled the country. Allowing residents to participate in the external purchase of debts to be converted by the central bank into domestic interest-bearing liabilities is a means of capturing the external discount and sharing it between residents and the central bank. This has in fact been done with success in Chile. But once again, this will be particularly attractive only when interest rates in the debtor country are not far in excess of rates on external debt and when foreign exchange is plentiful. Such a combination would be rare.

The scope for market-related debt reduction schemes is limited. The secondary market for developing-country debt may present opportunities, however, for coordinated intervention through an international debt-reduction facility.

A Debt-Service-Reduction Facility
International coordination can help developing countries capture the secondary market discount while allowing creditors to achieve more secure portfolios. The Task Force believes that an official international facility, capitalized and guaranteed by the industrial countries, can play a role in a fair and constructive solution of the debt problem. This idea has flourished since Professor Peter Kenen of Princeton University first put forth a proposal for a debt discount facility in 1983. The Task Force believes that there are two versions of this idea that warrant consideration.

The Market-Maker Role. Some officials have suggested using a market maker or facilitator (a bureau of information, so to speak) to encourage more banks and countries to avail themselves of the opportunities offered by the secondary market. Debtor countries would benefit to the extent that they capture a part of the discount associated with a refinancing. (The Mexican debt conversion scheme of 1987-88 is an example of a situation in which a facilitator might have been useful.) It could help develop financially sustainable debt-refinancing techniques, explore new means of satisfying regulatory requirements (and urge them on regulators and accounting boards), and suggest techniques by which debtors could more securely guarantee debt-service performance.

While in principle private financial markets can be very helpful here, the Task Force believes a more visible and active official participation may be needed. Moreover, a voluntary market solution raises the "free rider" problem. Although a debt-service-reduction facility would ideally come about as a result of an agreement between creditors and debtors, that is unlikely to happen. If many banks were to participate, and as a result a significant debt-service reduction were to take place, any individual bank would have an incentive not to participate. The debt-service reduction of all the participants frees resources to pay the *full* claims of all those who stay out. As a result, as the Mexican auction has already demonstrated, debt reduction as a market outcome will be insignificant.*

---

* *Frank E. Morris, speaking for himself and not for the Federal Reserve System in either joining with the majority or dissenting, dissents:*

It is misleading to associate the so-called free rider problem with the failure of the Mexican auction. Many banks that would have been happy to reduce the size of their Mexican commitment found, upon analysis, that the plan had

(Continued on page 16)

To avoid the free rider problem, *the Task Force recommends that legislators and regulators in creditor countries take the initiative to assure participation by a significant share of the creditors.* Such participation can be achieved by creating incentives in the form of regulatory advantages: for example, by stipulating an extended period during which loss provisions can be made on the side of capital retirements and losses can be carried forward for tax purposes. Alternatively, regulators and legislators could impose costly capital and tax rules for nonparticipating banks.*

There is also a free rider problem with respect to governments. Much of the discussion about debt-reduction facilities has focused on commercial bank claims. But even in the major debtor countries, official claims amount to more than a quarter of total debt. Therefore, it is entirely appropriate to ask what treatment official debts should receive. In these cases, *the Task Force believes that a distinction should be made among official debts, between claims of the World Bank and the International Monetary Fund (IMF) on one hand and direct government debts on the other.* Such a distinction is appropriate because a write-down of World Bank claims would potentially harm the interests of much poorer countries.

A Debt Guarantee and Refinancing Trust. The Task Force recommends, therefore, a more comprehensive program for refinancing developing-country debt, in which *the refinancing facility would buy, at significant discounts, commercial banks' claims on developing countries. These debts would then be renegotiated with the debtor to pass on those discounts.*

(Continued from page 15)
little to offer. By accepting a major write-down of their principal claim, they could guarantee repayment of the balance twenty years hence. However, their standing with respect to interest payments was unchanged and their claim to interest payments was substantially reduced. Furthermore, the resulting bonds, since they bore a below-market rate of interest, could not be sold except at a further sizable discount. If the banks had been offered the bonds of our proposed Debt Guarantee and Refinancing Trust, there would have been many takers at even larger discounts.

Richard N. Cooper and R. T. McNamar concur with Mr. Morris.
* Frank E. Morris dissents:
The capacity of individual banks to participate in debt conversion schemes varies widely. Thus any mandatory participation plan could be destabilizing to the financial system. Participation must remain a voluntary matter.

The renegotiated debt would involve a present value equal to or slightly in excess of the obligation incurred by the trust toward the commercial bank, but the timing and contingencies of payments would be arranged flexibly to foster development.

The facility should be affiliated with an existing international agency, most appropriately with the World Bank. In this way, existing expertise and experience could most easily be tapped.

To have significant impact on the world debt problem, the facility would need substantial support from creditor governments. Capital subscriptions—after several years of phase-in—must be sufficient to convert a significant fraction of debt into guaranteed bonds. This commitment should be shared by developed countries.

The Task Force recognizes that this larger role for the facility poses a difficulty: taxpayers in developed countries would have to underwrite the default risk. Even if the renegotiated debt has a present value equal to the trust's commitment toward the initial creditors, there is a risk of nonperformance. In that case, taxpayers would have to absorb the risk, but it might be reduced to a very small probability if the trust is structured in a way that it shares disproportionately in favorable outcomes in the debtor countries. It must be kept in mind, however, that there is no way for taxpayers to avoid risk completely, since their governments guarantee to maintain the payment system. Hence the relevant question concerns the nature and size of the risk. It is better for taxpayers to bear some default risk rather than be burdened with unconditional subsidies of banks or debtors.

An important advantage of a trust is that it can influence debtor country policy by making participation conditional on reform measures. The leverage for a new, more productive conditionality is twofold. First, there are direct interest savings that come from debt reduction. Second, the trust could subordinate its claims to flows of new money that would be part of an approved reconstruction program. By removing the seniority of existing debt (and that of banks that hold out), the trust would help reverse the pattern of international transfers and allow a resumption of development finance.*

---

* *Frank E. Morris and Richard N. Cooper dissent:*
The implication that granting seniority to new loans would generate sizable new voluntary flows of development money seems unrealistic to us. The banks

(Continued on page 18)

Banks too should benefit from the facility. Smaller banks, eager to remove Third World debt from their books, can be expected to use the liquidity the facility would add to secondary debt markets to convert their debt to guaranteed bonds. With these banks out of the picture, the free rider program would be reduced. Major creditor banks would find it easier to negotiate new lending agreements.

As described above, the trust would seek to achieve a reduction in debt principal and hence debt-service requirements. An alternative is a fund that guarantees interest payments rather than principal. The trust might, for example, guarantee over a horizon of three years interest payments on the external debt of a country. In exchange for the guarantee, there would be a significant reduction of the amount of interest due. This might be done by balancing current cash flows—the fund would receive reduced funds from debtors and pass these on to banks that are protected by the guarantee.

The fund could also increase the flexibility of the debtors' service flows by assuming assets and liabilities with different payment schedules. Under such a system, reduced guaranteed payments would be made to the banks on a predetermined time schedule. But the debtor countries' payments, while reduced in present value, might have a more flexible time schedule, taking into account the current ability to pay. Once again, the only subsidy element in this scheme is the guarantee, which could be offset by special fees levied on countries in particularly favorable conditions.

The Role of the Taxpayer

The Task Force strongly believes that it is pointless to argue that the taxpayer in industrial countries cannot and should not participate in any

---

(Continued from page 17)
are not likely to loan substantial amounts of new money, because their new claims are senior to their old ones. The market would not look kindly upon any bank that chose to do so. Bonds might be sold with a senior claim to bank debt, but only at interest rates that the debtor nations would view as unacceptably high.

There will be no large flows of voluntary private development debt until the creditworthiness of the debtor countries is restored. In the meantime, new money flows will be limited to trade credit, equity investment, and loans by governmental organizations. For now, the primary emphasis must be on reducing the servicing burden of the old debt.

solution to the debt problem. The taxpayer is already participating, because bank losses have tax consequences, as do the trade and foreign policy implications of the debt crisis. The issue therefore is how taxpayer dollars can best secure economic, financial, and political interests. As suggested in the discussion of the debt facility, the Task Force believes that the taxpayers' interests are best served when creditor country governments guarantee debt-restructuring arrangements that are combined with policy reforms in the debtor countries. The Task Force does not believe that taxpayers' money should be used for outright subsidies. One suggestion of particular concern envisages a much more ambitious role for the debt facility. It would have the facility combine its intermediary and refinancing roles with outright subsidies. For example, taxpayers in developing countries would relieve the debtor countries of some future interest payments to the trust. Such subsidized financing is aid, and thus must be balanced against the special needs of countries much poorer than the main debtors. Likewise, using the World Bank as a financial resource, filling the gap left by the banks, is an indirect way of using taxpayer resources.

Taxpayer involvement would be most obvious, however, if a major financial crisis were precipitated by an uncontrolled development on the debt front. This could lead to financial distress throughout the world economy. Although this appears unlikely, there is enough financial vulnerability in financial systems today to take it seriously. The damage to the industrialized countries' economies and the resulting consequences for taxpayers would be long lasting.

Currently, taxpayers guarantee debt indirectly through the explicit and implicit commitments of their governments and central banks to shore up the financial system in a crisis. *The role of the taxpayer should not be expanded to make up bank losses nor to grant subsidies on the basis of debt burdens. Rather, indirect guarantees should be made direct and placed in the context of wider reforms.* The taxpayer, as well as the debtor countries and the banks, is better served by a system that uses guarantees as conditions of measures to promote economic development than by a system of unconditional bailouts.

Recommendations

The primary concern of the members of the Task Force is the need for development finance: it is critical to the economic and political stabili-

ty and progress of the debtors and, hence, ultimately to the prosperity of the creditors. The Task Force's recommendations are all aimed at increasing the likelihood of renewed growth in the debtor nations.

There is considerable uncertainty about the economic consequences for debtor countries, for commercial banks, and for the world economy of the current debt management strategy. A confrontation or crisis in world financial markets is not imminent or inevitable, and the members of the Task Force do not rule out the possibility that the present debt strategy might work out. This is especially the case if favorable developments in the world economy and unusual patience and success in debtor countries combine to allow debt service under conditions of growth and financial stability. But we believe that it is only prudent to take constructive steps now, before uncontrolled developments, possibly in contexts of confrontation, make them difficult if not impossible.

The Task Force has made a number of recommendations that can be put in place immediately, as well as other recommendations that will take time to implement. In terms of the former, *the Task Force strongly recommends that efforts be undertaken immediately to introduce interest capitalization and local currency interest recycling, as means of reconciling the requirements of investment and growth in debtor countries with the rights of creditors.* The situation of debtor countries requires a departure from contracts as negotiated in the past. Debtor countries should be given the leeway of temporary suspension of transfers abroad. But *the members of the Task Force recommend that, in exchange, the debtors commit themselves to undertake demanding policy reforms in order to enhance significantly their long-term ability to service debts.*

The preferred mechanism for implementing a recycling of interest is mutual agreement between a debtor country and its creditors. Creditor country governments can play an important role in this context by having their own claims treated similarly to those of other creditors. They should initiate discussions on interest recycling with countries that are in a good position to implement such programs, notably Mexico. They should also develop mechanisms within the IMF and the World Bank that would make recycling a systematic part of long-term adjustment programs. They must find ways to allow banks to overcome the regulatory and tax consequences of an interest recycling as smoothly as possible.

The members of the Task Force have chosen not to spell out the details of how local currency interest recycling would take place. However, it might be accomplished in the most decentralized form, with each creditor receiving payments and deciding how to use them for maximum advantage. Alternatively, *investment funds* might be set up to collect and invest the payments received by creditors. The only concern is that institutional arrangements should not become a means of reducing the profitability of the captive resources nor the quality of the domestic investments they finance. Local currency recycling is particularly well suited for the major debtors—Mexico, Brazil, the Philippines, Argentina, and Venezuela—where there are relatively good domestic capital markets.

The long-term recommendations of the Task Force cannot be put in place as easily, because they require legislative action. *Chief among these is the Task Force's recommendation for a debt facility that would reduce debt burdens by renegotiating debts with banks and with the debtors.* If such a facility can restructure debts, not only by reducing their present value but also by deferring interest payments and making them more contingent and flexible, major progress would be achieved. Flexibility in debt service requires that governments provide incentives for participation by regulatory and tax concessions. The passage of the Omnibus Trade Act of 1988 in the United States, and with it the endorsement by Congress of one version of the debt facility, is a promising step in the right direction.

It might be tempting to see the facility as an alternative for those countries that do not wish to subscribe to the rigorous adjustment discipline that recycling would demand. But that would poorly serve the general interest. Within the dealings of a debt-reduction facility, *a serious program of adjustment should be the sine qua non of debt restructuring.*

There has been a great deal of ink spilled on solutions to the debt crisis, but the Task Force believes that far too little of it has been informed by a realistic assessment of what is possible. There is no doubt that it is critical to encourage the investment of new money, but without a resolution of the old-money problem there is little chance this will occur. Furthermore, no solution will succeed that does not take into consideration the interests of all parties. Implementation of the recommendations of the Task Force could help to stanch the outflow of resources from the debtor countries and pave the way for renewed development.

Notes

1. In fact, of the claims on the major problem debtors, only 19 percent represent claims by U.S. banks; 54 percent is owed to banks in other countries, notably Japan, West Germany, and the United Kingdom.

2. For the debt-ridden sub-Saharan countries, the share of debt to official agencies is 74 percent. Their debt problems call for an agreement by creditor countries' governments on how best to offer debt relief. But for the major problem debtors elsewhere, the official share is only 27 percent.

Appendix to the Report

Table 1
Debt Ratios in Heavily Indebted Countries [a]
(percent)

	1978–81	1982	1983	1984	1985	1986	1987
Debt/GNP	33.6	45.6	56.3	56.7	57.6	59.6	58.0
Debt/Exports	186.7	254.2	286.4	267.4	282.3	335.6	317.9
Debt Service/GNP	5.8	7.9	8.0	7.8	7.5	6.9	6.2
Debt Service/Exports	32.4	43.9	40.6	36.9	36.9	39.1	34.1
Interest/GNP	2.7	4.8	5.4	5.4	5.1	4.5	3.9
Interest/Exports	15.3	26.9	27.2	25.4	25.2	25.3	21.4

Source: World Bank, "World Bank Operational Strategy in the Heavily Indebted Middle Income Countries," March 9, 1988.
a. Countries include the Baker 15—Argentina, Bolivia, Brazil, Chile, Colombia, Equador, Ivory Coast, Mexico, Morocco, Nigeria, Peru, the Philippines, Uruguay, Venezuela, Yugoslavia—plus Costa Rica and Jamaica.

Table 2
Recent Economic Performance and Minimum Goals
for Heavily Indebted Countries
(percent of GDP)

	1978–81[a]	1983–86	1987	Minimum Goal
GDP Growth				
(% per annum)	4.3	1.3	2.5	5.0
Investment and Savings				
Investment	25.0[b]	19.0	19.4	24.0
Domestic Savings	21.0[b]	17.4	17.8	20.0
Net Capital Inflow	4.0	1.6	1.6	4.0
Balance of Payments				
Noninterest				
Current Account	–1.3	3.4	2.3	0.0
Interest Due	–2.7	–5.0	–3.9	–4.0
Finance Required	4.0	1.6	1.6	4.0
Memorandum				
Interest (billion $)	21.4	38.0	32.1	—
Net Capital Inflow				
(billion $)	31.5	12.1	13.0	—

Source: Columns 1, 2, and 3 adapted from World Bank, "World Bank Operational Strategy in the Heavily Indebted Middle Income Countries," March 9, 1988; Minimum Goals proposed by the Task Force.

　a. Figures for 1982 are not given because of the transitional nature of that year.

　b. Approximation.

Table 3
External Finance: Requirements and Sources
(billions $ annum)

	1982–84	1985–87	Minimum Required
Net Financing Required [a]	20.0	10.9	36.0
Sources			
Private Direct Investment	4.2	3.4	3.0
Change in Short-term Credit	–12.7	–9.5	—
Bilateral Transfers and Credit	3.2	2.6	3.0
World Bank, IDA, and Other Development Banks	3.7	4.2	4.0
Remainder (Financed by Private Creditors, IMF, and Others) [b]	21.6	10.2	26.0

Source: World Bank, ''World Bank Operational Strategy in the Heavily Indebted Middle Income Countries,'' March 9, 1988.

a. Includes addition to reserves.

b. 1982–87 figures include net International Monetary Fund financing, medium- and long-term private credit, capital not elsewhere included, reserve valuation adjustments, and errors and omissions.

BACKGROUND PAPER

by

Rudiger Dornbusch

Chapter 1
Introduction

Several Latin American countries are in desperate straits seven years after the international debt crisis began making newspaper headlines. A number of these countries remain illiquid and perhaps even insolvent. They lack the foreign exchange resources for timely service of their debts. Since their creditors are not prepared to lend them the extra resources needed for the payment of interest, the governments of the industrialized countries and the international financial institutions are managing a system of involuntary debt service and involuntary lending. Loans are kept current and even productive by limited "new money" contributions by commercial banks and by severe adjustment programs that have brought about austerity through cutbacks in government spending and in imports. But this solution brings with it political intervention by the creditors in enforcing debt service. The whole system is kept afloat by the determination of the creditors to avoid collapse by providing creative and plentiful financing when essential, as for example in the recent $3.5 billion emergency bridge loan to Mexico or the ongoing operation to keep Argentina afloat. So far this approach has worked: unlike the 1930s, outright default has, at least for the moment, been averted. Brazil has come back to the international system after more than a year of moratorium, but this hardly conceals the fact that a growing number of smaller debtor countries are in a quiet, de facto state of moratorium.

The number of countries forced to reschedule their debts because of debt-servicing difficulties rose dramatically from three in 1978—Peru, Jamaica, and Turkey—to eight in mid-1982. Soon it became easier to list the debtor nations that were not in trouble than those that were. Far from being an isolated instance, debt problems are common enough now to have a special category of developing countries known for their threatening debt difficulties, the "15 heavily indebted" identified by former Secretary of the Treasury James Baker.[1]

The Mexican moratorium of August 1982 ushered in the new phase in bank lending to the debtor countries: involuntary lending and harsh adjustment programs in place of overly abundant lending and free spending. During this new phase, since debts cannot be serviced, rescheduling of interest and principal is now the rule. In 1981 only six countries had to undergo a restructuring of their debt; by 1985 the number had risen to fifteen; and in 1987 there were thirteen financial packages already concluded, with another nine still under negotiation. In the period from 1983 to 1987 more than $300 billion of debt was restructured because of debtors' inability to service the claims.[2]

Moreover, the past seven years have not been marked by any lessening of debt problems. While many countries have made serious efforts to follow their adjustment programs, none has again become creditworthy, which means that a return of voluntary lending is definitely not on the horizon. On the contrary, creditor banks are wearying of involuntary lending. The question now is how to solve the dilemma, keeping banks intact while giving relief to debtors—and how to do this without placing the burden on the U.S. taxpayer.

The current debt-service process was expected to be self-correcting. Favorable conditions in the world economy and the beneficial effects of adjustment programs on the part of debtors were to bring about an improvement in creditworthiness that would, in time, mean a return to voluntary lending. That remains the expectation, but it has not happened. Although the oil price decline improved the situation of Korea and Brazil, while dramatically worsening that of Mexico, the improvements have not met expectations. In fact, a return to voluntary lending is very remote to judge by the large discounts in the secondary market for the debts of the less developed countries (LDCs).

Basically, there is still a debt crisis. Not only has there been no steady improvement, but there is now concern that conditions may deteriorate: Over the past few years, the trade balance of Latin debtors turned toward a significant surplus, allowing Latin America to pay a large share of the interest liabilities. But at the same time, their inflation rates increased sharply and their investment declined sharply. For a brief period, a cut in investment may be a reasonable response to the crisis, but when it is prolonged, it inevitably leads to trouble.

Although there have been no major political crises yet, politicians and policymakers in debtor countries are concerned that ultimately their citizens will bear the costs for prolonging what seems to be a totally unreasonable decapitalization of their economies.

Economic conditions in debtor countries have deteriorated sharply (see Table 1-1): per capita growth has turned negative, investment has declined sharply, and inflation has become an overriding concern. In fact, first Bolivia and then Argentina and Brazil have come to experience conditions of hyperinflation. It is easy to point to the renewed rise of Peronism in Argentina, the political shift in Venezuela and Ecuador, and the challenge to the established rule of the PRI in Mexico as events closely related to countries' poor performance as a result of debt problems.

The reversal of the normal flow of lending from capital-abundant to capital-poor countries is not only occurring via the official route of involuntary debt service, but it is reinforced by private capital flight. Capital is fleeing from countries where involuntary debt service strains public finance, leaving behind the poorer groups. They ultimately foot the bill not only for mismanagement at the outset of the debt crisis (which may have been for their benefit) but also for the extra debts and adjustments incurred to finance the capital outflow on the part of the wealthier groups in society. This pattern of redistribution will become political dynamite inviting outright default. Although no populist government has yet gained power dramatizing this issue, it is clear that in Brazil, Mexico, and Argentina it is an issue hovering below the surface. Brazil, until recently, and Peru are in fact in a state of moratorium, 1930s-style.

Even before Citicorp made its decision to set aside more reserves against potential losses from loans to the debtor countries (a move that was soon followed by other banks), large banks in the United States were

Table 1-1
The Economic Deterioration of Debtor Countries
(Group of Fifteen Heavily Indebted Countries)
(percent per year)

	Per Capita Growth	Investment/ GDP Ratio	Inflation
1970–81	2.7	25.1	39
1982–88	– 0.7	17.9	149

Source: IMF, *World Economic Outlook,* April 1986 and October 1988.

becoming increasingly disenchanted with Federal Reserve and Treasury pressure to keep up lending. They would prefer a more substantial takeover by the taxpayer, either overtly or under the cover of expanded loans and guarantees from international agencies. The problem is aggravated by the increasing unwillingness of small banks to participate in new rounds of lending. Their refusal puts pressure on loan discounts and thus highlights the fact that loans are traded significantly below par.

Trade issues play an enormous part in the crisis. Debtor countries have to run trade surpluses to earn foreign exchange. They have achieved these surpluses by large depreciations of their currencies to increase their competitiveness, by restrictions on imports, and by an expansion in exports. This shift in trade practices, though, is perceived as a threat. Protectionism in the industrialized countries, and specifically in the United States when an overly strong dollar was doing even more damage, has therefore become an important political issue. Since 1986, protectionist sentiment in the United States has been dampened, in part as a result of dollar depreciation. But even so, the rapid growth of imports from debtor countries continues to be an active issue for trade policy.

The Analytic Framework

Before examining the origins of the 1982 debt crisis, it may be useful to set out an analytic framework. The balance-of-payments account provides such a basic framework, involving relations that are true always and anywhere by accounting definition, thus providing an objective conceptual setting. A debt problem occurs when a debtor cannot meet scheduled payments for interest or amortization. Here the concentration is on interest payments, although a bunching of maturities and a resulting inability to meet principal payments were certainly part of the 1982 debt crisis.

It is helpful to separate the current account into the noninterest current account, which includes trade in goods and in all services except interest payments on the external debt, and interest payments. The separation emphasizes the special role of financing interest payments around which the debt crisis revolves today. These interest payments can be financed either by new money from banks (increasingly difficult to obtain) or by noninterest surpluses of debtor countries (very costly to bring about).

The noninterest current account deficit is often called the *net resource transfer,* since it measures the net imports of goods and services.

Noninterest deficits are the normal pattern for developing countries in which saving is low relative to investment. Noninterest deficits are the channel through which resources are transferred from rich to poor countries to support capital formation, growth, and progress in the developing world.[3] Private and public lending forms the financial counterpart.

Table 1-2 reveals the shift in the noninterest current account from a string of deficits until 1982 to a series of surpluses. In the period up to 1982, both interest payments and the deficit in the noninterest current account need financing and therefore are reflected in a rapidly rising debt. Since 1983 a large part of the interest on the debts has been paid out of surpluses in the noninterest current account. As a result, the increase in external debt is sharply reduced but still rises. The surpluses are not large enough to completely cover interest payments as well as the financing of capital flight and buildup of international reserves by debtor countries.

A current account deficit must be financed by a net capital inflow, which includes direct investment inflows, long-term portfolio investment, official lending, and lending by private creditors. It is important, though, to distinguish gross and net flows. The net capital inflow in the balance of payments represents the excess of new borrowing over amortization of debts coming due and capital outflows. A new loan, the proceeds of which help pay off a maturing debt, does not represent a net capital inflow, nor does an increase in external debt that is a result of capital flight by domestic residents.

A debt crisis arises when the interest payments a country owes increase, the deficit in the noninterest current account grows, and creditors

Table 1-2
The Current Account Deficit and External Debt:
The Fifteen Heavily Indebted Countries (billion $)

	Noninterest Current Account	Interest Payments	External Debt
1978–81 Average	– 8.9	23.1	248
1981	– 12.9	37.1	332
1982	– 5.3	44.4	380
1983–87 Average	33.7	41.9	432
1988	32.7	42.8	484

Source: IMF, *World Economic Outlook,* April 1986 and October 1988.

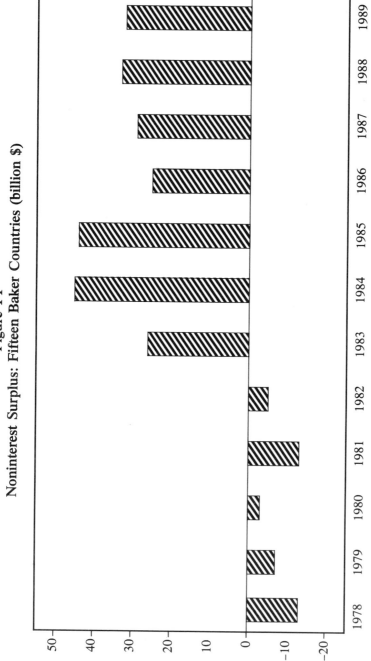

Figure 1-1

Noninterest Surplus: Fifteen Baker Countries (billion $)

Source: IMF, *World Economic Outlook*, April 1986, October 1986, and October 1988.

become unwilling to further increase their exposure.[4] The financing equation then no longer adds up. Something must give. When a debt crisis occurs and arrears or outright default is not the answer, creditors are often coerced into involuntary lending and debtors undergo adjustment programs to turn their noninterest deficits into surpluses. Theoretically, an adequate program could reestablish creditworthiness. Then debtors would have noninterest surpluses that would finance the interest payments. But there could still be a part of interest payments financed by net capital inflows or new money.

The essential distinction between precrisis and postcrisis is the shift of the net resource balance to a point where debtor countries are making net resource transfers to creditor countries. That is not a sustainable solution because, to work, the shift to a noninterest surplus must involve a budget improvement, a cut in investment, or a cut in consumption. Unless a rise in saving is possible, the counterpart of the noninterest surplus must be a reduction in investment or cuts in the budget. Both are controversial because both involve a cut in the standard of living.

Today more than half of interest payments is generated by trade surpluses of the debtor countries (see Figure 1-1). The policy issues behind those surpluses—budget correction, cuts in the standard of living, trade policy conflicts—are half the debt crisis. The other half concerns the question of who will lend the interest that is not earned by trade surpluses.

Chapter 2
The Origins of the
1982 Debt Crisis

The 1982 debt crisis was the result of a combination of events:

• The downturn of the world economy that resulted in sharply increased interest rates, falling commodity prices, and stagnation in the markets for manufactured exports;

• The rise in oil prices in 1973-74 and 1978-79, which helped bring about the downturn of the world economy. The rise created payment problems for oil importers but did not, surprisingly, make things better for most oil exporters;

• The debtor countries' mismanagement of their economies, overvaluation of their currencies, and failure to use external resources efficiently;

• The overlending of money, without sufficient investigation of the possibility of credit risk, by the commercial bankers.

It is difficult, if not impossible, to assign a precise share of the blame for what happened in 1982 to any one of these events. Clearly, each affected the others, and just as clearly, responsibility for the crisis must fall on debtors and creditors alike, since without lending there would have been no borrowing, and vice versa. Assigning blame is, in any event, far less interesting or useful than trying to determine why all the countries involved, each of which has a very different economic structure, experienced debt-service problems at the same time.

Changes in the World Economy Preceding the Crisis

Debtor countries are quite right in emphasizing that their ability to service their debts was adversely affected by the deterioration in world economic conditions. They point to the combination of falling export revenues (caused by recession and declining commodity prices) and sharp increases in the cost of debt service (caused primarily by the extraordinary increase in market interest rates due to the shift toward tight money in the United States).

From 1976 to 1980, inflation in the United States reached double-digit levels as oil prices doubled and the dollar collapsed. The Federal Reserve responded with a sharp turn toward tight money. This increase in interest rates in the United States played a critical role in the crisis because the higher rates were passed on to debtors, especially in Latin America, whose floating rates were tied to U.S. market rates.[1]

Fiscal correction and tight money in the United States led to a sharp slowdown in the growth of world income and spending. While growth in the industrial countries had been in the 3 to 4 percent range between 1968 and 1979, it slowed to less than 2 percent in 1980-81 and to –0.4 percent in 1982. The result was lower commodity prices and a reduction in the growth in demand for manufactures exports from developing countries.

The real price of commodities (excluding petroleum), deflated by the unit value of manufactures imported by developing countries, declined by one-third between 1980 and 1985, thus dramatically reducing the export revenue of commodity-exporting countries. Of course, this was not the first time commodity prices had declined sharply in real terms. There had been sharp declines after rises in the 1950s and the 1970s, but those corrections did not bring about a crisis.

The role of oil prices is part of the picture, and oil pricing was dramatically changed by the oil shocks of the 1970s. In the two years immediately preceding the crisis, the role oil played in the economy of a country depended on whether it was a net importer or exporter. Brazil, for example, imports oil and exports commodities. Thus the country was caught by adverse price developments on both the import and export side. The real price of oil doubled, raising import costs, while declining prices for commodities reduced export revenue. Korea, on the other hand, was in a more balanced position, hurt by increased oil prices, but gaining as a net commodity importer from the lower prices of commodities. Finally, a net oil exporter and (nonoil) commodity-importing country like Mexico gained from higher oil prices.

The net effect of oil and commodity price movements in the period 1978-82 can be determined by examining the changes in the cumulative terms of trade for the period. There was a large deterioration in the terms of trade of net oil-importing countries (–20.1), which was matched on the plus side by the increase (18.0) for the net oil exporters. Neither change is unexpected. Interestingly, when the terms of trade for countries with recent debt-servicing problems are examined, there is no significant change (–0.9 percent) because the group includes Mexico and Nigeria (oil exporters) as well as Brazil (oil importer).

Mismanagement by Debtors

In virtually every debtor country, mismanagement played a significant part in the debt crisis. In most, at some point in the late 1970s, the governments turned to economic policies that encouraged excessive spending and/or capital flight. The result was a payments deficit that had to be financed by foreign loans. The loans were not "productive"; that is, they were not used to finance growth. Accordingly, the increased debt never came close to being matched by an increased capacity to service debts. If the increased debt had been put into productive investments, servicing that debt would not have presented a major difficulty.

Because so much of the borrowed money ended up being used for the purchase of consumer goods or was shipped abroad by worried citizens, the legacy of the 1978-82 policy mistakes is a continuing, serious debt-service problem.

The mismanagement that brought about the problems was different in each country. In Argentina, the government overvalued the currency in a mistaken attempt to stop inflation, an attempt that brought about a rapid and large flight of capital. Chile also attempted to reduce inflation by controlling exchange rates, but because Chile had liberalized trade, not the capital account, as part of its economic policy, the public began to spend heavily on consumer goods. Mexico also suffered from massive capital flight because of an overvaluation of its currency, but in Mexico the cause was strong economic expansion combined with a fixed exchange rate. Only in Brazil did increased indebtedness, at least in the early 1970s, have a substantial counterpart in the form of investment.*

Of course, in the long run, it makes little difference which particular form of mismanagement caused the enormous buildup of gross exter-

---

* The Appendix at the end of this chapter presents a more detailed examination of the domestic mismanagement in these four countries.

nal debt. The interesting problem is to identify what part mismanagement rather than accident played in the crisis. It may help answer the question, Why did so many countries, at the same time, incur such large increases?

Eduardo Wiesner, a director of the International Monetary Fund, concluded in 1985:

> No other set of factors explains more of the debt crisis than the fiscal deficits incurred by most of the major countries in Latin America. Although there were other factors that were relevant, I have no doubt that the main problem was excessive public (and private) spending that was financed by both easy domestic credit policies and by ample resources from abroad. The world recession and high interest rates in international markets aggravated the crisis, but I do not believe they created it. What actually happened was that previous domestic policies had made economies more vulnerable to exogenous factors.[2]

A statement by Ciro DeFalco of the U.S. Treasury goes even further in singling out domestic mismanagement as the cause of the debt crisis:

> . . . the debt crisis just did not happen in 1982 or was not the result of the increase in the oil price shock of '79-80 or the rise in the dollar exchange rate. The cause of the debt crisis had its domestic origins in the economic policies of the debtor countries and so what we are seeing and what we will continue to see is a change in these policies—budget deficits, excessive government spending, government interference in the markets, price controls and so on.[3]

The official view that mismanagement played an overriding part in the debt crisis formed the basis for the adjustment strategy imposed by the industrialized countries. The first step, those in charge of adjustment said, was straightening out the domestic policies of the debtor countries. They believed that world economic recovery and a carefully structured process for handling rescheduling would do the rest.

This is not an attempt to suggest that the domestic economic policies of the debtor nations were anything short of shocking. But at the same time, there is no reason to suggest that those policies triggered the crisis. The policies were as shocking in 1980 or 1981 as they were in 1982. Mismanagement helped create the preconditions, but it is difficult to believe that a debt crisis would have occurred if interest rates had not increased and if the recession of 1981-82 had not happened—and if the banks had not been so eager to lend.

Overlending

Looking back, it is easy to say that the commercial banks lent far too much to the debtor countries. But why did they do it? Was it because they were unaware that a debt crisis might take place? Or was the crisis brought about by a conjunction of altogether unusual and unpredictable events that caught debtors and creditors alike by surprise? And, if they did anticipate a crisis, did they go ahead and lend anyway because they were confident that they could collect sovereign debt (from the debtors or the U.S. taxpayers)?

The last question is likely to remain unanswered until, if ever, some of the bankers involved write their memoirs. But there is some information available that might help determine if the crisis was a surprise.

The records of 1980-81 do not indicate that there were strong warnings about the coming problem, although some literature by the Group of Thirty, the International Monetary Fund (IMF), and the Bank for International Settlements (BIS) indicates that there was some concern about the problem. For example, the IMF put the issue in the following terms:

> In aggregate terms, notwithstanding its rapid increase in recent years, outstanding total, non-oil developing country indebtedness measured in relation to such variables as GDP, or foreign reserves is broadly comparable to the level of the early 1970s; there is an increase, however, in the real burden of debt service. Furthermore, both the scale of the prospective imbalances and the incremental demand for private financing are smaller in relation to the size of financial markets than they were in 1973-74. It appears, therefore, that a continuation of recent growth rates in international bank lending would be sufficient, through 1981, to accommodate aggregate demand from developing country borrowers. The particular situation and prospects for an individual country, however, will tend to influence a bank's perception of that country's creditworthiness. While several countries face potentially serious debt problems, the severity of such problems could be significantly alleviated by the adoption of considerably strengthened adjustment and debt management policies.[4]

A survey of one hundred international banks by the Group of Thirty included the question: "Do you think that a generalized debt problem affecting developing countries is likely to emerge, and if so in what way would it emerge?" There were fifteen "yes" responses, seventy-two respondents answered "no," and another thirteen said "possibly." Among the reasons given for the high level of confidence expressed by the respondents was:

. . . that the highly concentrated exposure of international banks in some areas of Latin America and Asia would cause those banks to "take very determined steps indeed" to ensure that the borrowers maintained their viability.[5]

Thus it is clear that the debt difficulties were, as of 1981, apparently considered isolated problems of individual countries, not unlike the situation in Turkey or Zaire throughout the late 1970s. No one, at least publicly, anticipated the almost generalized rescheduling of 1982–88, and even less outright moratoria.

This failure to anticipate the crisis reveals a peculiar lack of awareness of history, or a determination to ignore it. The historical record indicates that every so often there is a generalized debt crisis. They were common in the nineteenth century; then, in the 1920s and 1930s, almost every country in Latin America—as well as many European countries—defaulted.

In 1938, Cleona Lewis summarized the interwar experience with foreign bonds in the following terms:

Of the existing foreign bonds that were originally issued here during the prosperous twenties, around 35 to 40 percent are now in default. In addition, payment has been suspended on practically all of the foreign government obligations that are held by the United States government. The enthusiasm with which the nation viewed its rapidly expanding foreign assets in 1929 and earlier years has disappeared. Many investors, acting through protective committees, are negotiating with their foreign debtors, hoping that satisfactory terms can be arranged for the resumption of payments. Many others have sold their defaulted foreign bonds for what they could get, and since then have restricted their security purchases to the issues of American borrowers.[6]

Why Was the Debt Problem Allowed to Turn into a Crisis?

The most plausible explanation for the failure to see the crisis coming was offered in a paper by Guttentag and Herring; they named the problem "disaster myopia."[7] What happens is, lenders do not have precise information about the probability of a generalized debt crisis. If each debt crisis is caused by events that can be considered unusual, the less likely the lenders are to put together any number of diffuse conditions as a possible package that will cause a new crisis.

The point of this interpretation is immediately evident from the discussion of the origins of the present debt crisis. If there was agreement, for example, on high interest rates as *the* cause, then it would be possible to create a formula for assessing risk using that information. But when there is no clear cause, but varying causes that interact with one another, the possibility of declaring that a crisis is coming is extraordinarily small. It cannot be ruled out, but it would not be predicted.

Appendix

The following analyses, while not exhaustive, will help convey the very large policy errors that were made by the debtor countries.

Argentina. In Argentina, capital flight rather than financing of current account deficits was behind the $2.7 billion increase in gross external debt in the 1978-82 period. Direct and long-term portfolio inflows provided another $7 billion in foreign exchange. But the cumulative current account deficit was only $11 billion. Capital flight is equal to the balance between foreign exchange receipts from borrowing and long-term capital inflows and the financing of the current account deficit (some $23 billion, which was used to finance capital flight). The large capital flight was a result of the ill-fated attempt to stop inflation by allowing the currency to become overvalued. Table 2A-1 provides some background.

In 1976, when the military overthrew the Peronist regime, inflation reached 600 percent. Although it was gradually brought down, in 1978-79 it was still near 200 percent. To achieve more rapid disinflation, Finance Minister Jose Alfredo Martinez de Hoz decided to rely on a scheme of gradually declining depreciation of the exchange rate, in the belief

Table 2A-1
Argentina's Macroeconomy: 1978-82

	1978	1979	1980	1981	1982
Inflation (% per year)	176	180	101	106	165
Budget Deficit (% of GDP)	10.1	9.0	11.3	16.4	17.2
Real Exchange Rate (Index 1975-83=100)	92	68	66	78	109

Source: R. Dornbusch, "External Debt, Budget Deficits, and Disequilibrium Exchange Rates," in *International Debt and the Developing Countries,* ed. G. Smith and J. Cuddington (Washington, D.C.: World Bank, 1985).

that the inflation-currency depreciation-inflation circle needed to be broken in order to cut inflation more dramatically. And so in December 1978, a pre-announced, gradually diminishing rate of depreciation that would achieve this result both directly via a reduction in cost pressure and indirectly by working on expectations was introduced.

Table 2A-1 shows that inflation indeed declined, but at the price of a significant real appreciation of the currency. The reduction in domestic wage and price inflation was much slower than the reduction in exchange depreciation. As a result, the currency became increasingly overvalued, but the government persisted in this policy until March 1981. From December 1978 to March 1981, the real exchange rate appreciated by fully 50 percent.

The sharp real appreciation was entirely unwarranted by the country's current account position. Interest rates in world markets had been increasing, and the terms of trade were deteriorating as a result of declining commodity prices. It was therefore apparent that real depreciation, not appreciation, was the appropriate direction for the currency. Not surprisingly, the increasing overvaluation had adverse effects on trade. But the chief effect was via the capital account. While trade was restricted, capital flows were entirely free. The government had liberalized the capital account (and domestic financial markets) to the point where it was possible to buy foreign exchange freely. With so obvious an overvaluation, the public quickly began to speculate against the government's exchange rate policy. From late 1979 until the scheme broke down, the government was forced to sell increasing amounts of dollars in the foreign exchange market, dollars borrowed in New York. The public who bought the underpriced dollars used them to buy assets abroad—deposits, certificates of deposit, real estate. Thus the net foreign assets of Argentina changed very little, but the government incurred a large external debt while the public acquired external assets.

In the end, the speculators carried the day. The exchange rate scheme collapsed, and the speculators realized their gains, leaving the treasury with the external debts.

Chile. Chile's debt accumulation also involved a plan to reduce inflation by exchange rate management. Following the overthrow of the Allende government, the military brought about a balanced budget and monetary control. Import protection ceased in an effort to open up the economy and make it more competitive and efficient. Inflation had dropped sharply from the hyperinflation level of 1973, but it never quite ended. By 1978, inflation was still near 40 percent. In order to speed up disinflation, the government moved in early 1978 to a fixed-dollar exchange rate. The currency was fixed at 39 pesos to the dollar and kept at that level until early 1982. Over the period, the *real* exchange rate appreciated by about 50 percent.

Chile's move to a fixed-dollar exchange rate did not work out because compulsory indexation of wages provided for automatic wage increases in an amount determined by past inflation. Thus, at the same time the country moved onto a fixed exchange rate, wage increases were given on the basis of the previous year's inflation of more than 40 percent. These wage increases implied increases in costs and in prices, which in turn meant a loss in competitiveness. And that process of backward-looking wage increases, entirely incompatible with a fixed exchange rate, continued for nearly four years. It should have been no surprise then that the exchange rate became increasingly overvalued. The growing overvaluation was accompanied by a gradual reduction in inflation. In that sense, at least, the policy was successful. But the problem, of course, was that, once inflation reached zero, the overvaluation had reached almost 50 percent compared to 1978. Falling real prices of copper and increased world interest rates were additional reasons why the exchange rate did not remain at a sustainable level.

The public quickly found out that foreign exchange was "on sale." But whereas in Argentina the capital account had been liberalized, making purchases of foreign assets the normal form of speculation, Chile's liberalization extended only to trade. Thus, with the prices of imported goods at an all-time low (in real terms), the public shifted massively into imported goods, particularly durables. At the peak of the speculation, in 1981, the volume of imports of consumer goods increased 75 percent over the preceding year, and automobile imports more than doubled in a single year. The current account deficit moved from an average of 6 percent of gross domestic product (GDP) in 1978-80 to 14.5 percent in 1981.

Mexico. The second round of oil price increases (1978-79) provided an apparently sound basis on which to engage in a growth strategy. Petroleum export revenue increased from only $1 billion in 1977 to $14 billion in 1981. But the increase in spending ran far ahead of the increase in revenues. The noninterest budget deficit, oil revenues notwithstanding, increased from 2 to more than 8 percent of GDP. The current account deteriorated even though oil revenues doubled every year (see Table 2A-2).

Table 2A-2
Mexico's Macroeconomy: 1977-81

	1977	1978	1979	1980	1981
Current Account Deficit (% of GDP)	2.3	3.1	4.1	4.4	5.8
Real Exchange Rate (1980-82=100)	93	94	98	104	114
Budget Deficit (% of GDP)	5.4	5.3	6.5	8.0	12.6

Source: Banco de Mexico.

The strong domestic expansion, combined with a fixed exchange rate, increased overvaluation, but the overvaluation never became as extreme as it had been in Chile and Argentina. Even so, it led to significant deterioration in the trade balance and to massive capital flight.

The capital flight was concentrated in the period 1981-82 in the final phase of the Lopez Portillo government. The deterioration in the external balance and the increasing difficulty in financing the deficit made it clear that an exchange crisis was around the corner. Large wage increases led everyone to expect a sharp increase in inflation that would be incompatible with the maintenance of a fixed exchange rate. With no restrictions on capital flows, what followed was a massive flight into the dollar. In fact, the capital flight would have been much larger had it not been for the existence of domestic dollar deposits in the banking system. These Mex-dollar accounts absorbed a good part of the speculation, although their holders ultimately did much worse than those who bought the real thing.

Estimates of the amount of capital flight from Mexico in 1978-82 differ. A recent study by J. Cuddington estimates a total of more than $25 billion, whereas Morgan Guaranty gives a higher number of $36 billion.[1] Whatever the exact number, there is no question that somewhere between 10 and 15 percent of GDP went abroad in these critical years. And the reason is exclusively mismanagement, since, unlike in the case of Argentina or Chile, there was no deterioration in external conditions until interest rates increased. On the contrary, the oil price increase had provided an extraordinary gain in real income and a potential improvement in the external balance.

Brazil. Brazil's gross external debt increased by nearly $50 billion in the period 1978-82. The cumulative current account over these years was approximately of equal magnitude. Overspending explains the debt accumulation, but the overspending was closely related to external shocks.

Because Brazil is an oil importer and a debtor, the increase in world oil prices of 1978-79 and the sharp rise in interest rates in 1980-81 vastly increased the current account deficit. The entire increase in Brazil's external debt in the 1978-82 period can be attributed to the increased cost of oil and the increased cost of debt service because of higher interest rates.[2] There is virtually no capital flight involved in the Brazilian debt accumulation.

The fact that external factors—oil and interest rates—explain the increased debt does not mean that there was no budget problem or policy mistake. The external shocks were simply absorbed by the budget and financed externally. The government did not pass the higher cost of debt service and petroleum in world markets on to households via increased real prices of public services and energy. As a result, the full effect of these disturbances appeared in the current account and in extra borrowing, as if the country had not gotten poorer. The failure to pass on to households the deterioration in real income thus explains the large increase in debt. It remains to be seen whether this was, in fact, a dramatic policy mistake. Of all the problem debtors, Brazil is perhaps the one today closest to being able to service its debt even at full employment.

Chapter 3
Adjustment to the Debt Crisis

In the immediate aftermath of the Mexican crisis of August 1982, the commercial banks, creditor governments, and the International Monetary Fund joined together to help solve the problems created by the debtor countries. They prescribed adjustment programs for each of the debtor countries that would bring about improvements in their current accounts, and they came through with new loans to see them through until the adjustment programs had their desired effects.

These actions on the part of the creditors were based on a number of assumptions. First, they believed that the debt crisis represented temporary illiquidity, not insolvency on the part of the debtor countries. Since the creditors thought that the debt crisis was temporary, and probably short term, it was clearly in their interest to help the debtors through the crisis rather than have them repudiate the debts or accept write-downs. It was one way to help guarantee that the debt would eventually be paid.

Of course, at the heart of the creditors' optimism was their belief that the world economy would improve, bringing about a rise in commodity prices, a resumption of sustained growth in the industrialized nations, and a reduction in interest rates, all of which would aid the debtor countries. In addition, once the debtors were restored to creditworthiness, not only would the debts be serviced, but a return to voluntary lending would be possible.

The debtor countries went along with adjustment, convinced by the creditor countries that the costs would be politically acceptable. And on first sight, adjustment appears a success: debts have been largely serviced, there have been no major debt riots, and with the exception of

Peru's suspension of debt service and Brazil's temporary moratorium, no highly visible unilateral action was taken. But, as already noted, a significant number of countries are in a quiet de facto state of nonperformance. And adjustment has not come without costs.

On the creditor side, the agreement between the banks and other creditors on how to proceed is rapidly eroding. In the debtor countries, adjustment has been responsible for a sharp reduction in per capita income, raging inflation, a collapse of new investments, and increasing difficulties in sustaining the refinancing of debt. Moreover, the debtors are unlikely to continue to accept further adjustment without visible rewards in the form of reduced interest burdens and long-term credit commitments.

The Adjustment Problems of Debtors[1]

Why has the shift in focus from borrowing to debt service been such a problem? In one sense the answer is quite straightforward: countries that once borrowed the resources needed for spending from official and private creditors (with little thought of how to service or even less repay the loans) are now limited to spending only their own income, which all too often proves to be very small. Shifting to debt service is complicated by two facts—the macroeconomics of earning foreign exchange and the political economy problem of finding extra budget resources for debt service.

The Reduction in Spending. Before the debt crisis, foreign loans supplemented domestic income, increasing spendable resources. Interest payments on loans were automatically provided in the form of new money, and principal was automatically rolled over. As long as the debt could be managed in this way, and as long as these countries had ready access to resources beyond those necessary to service the debt, spending ran high. Once credit rationing began in 1982, spending had to be limited almost to the level of income, with interest payments paid out of trade surpluses.

That is easier said than done. Once spending cuts were accepted, the issue of how to distribute the cut in spending among the government, consumption, and investment had to be decided. In the end, most of the cut took the form of reduced investment, but there was, of course, also some decline in consumption. The reason that a fall in investment was not enough has to do with two special features of the adjustment process. Cutting total demand ends up lowering output, income, and hence private spending, and just as involuntary debt service began, there was a deterioration in the world economy, requiring an extra adjustment in spending.

The Foreign Exchange Problem. Another issue in the adjustment to debt involves foreign exchange: the country needs to earn and pay dollars, not pesos. In other words, it must generate a trade surplus if it is to service its debt. The cut in spending will not only reduce import demand but free up goods for sale abroad. A sizable fraction of the expenditure cut will fall on domestic or nontradable goods, not tradables. The spending cut thus also creates unemployment rather than only potential foreign exchange earnings. Nor is it certain that increased supplies of tradable goods guarantee sales abroad. Other nations may deny access to markets, or if the goods are not homogeneous commodities, like cotton or copper, the prices of the goods exported will have to be cut if sales are to increase. Even then, unless demand is sufficiently responsive, total earnings may not increase.

To translate the spending cut into foreign exchange earnings, the debtor country must become more competitive. The gain in competitiveness in the home economy draws resources into the tradable-goods sector, making it possible to increase the production of these goods. Of course, the only way to gain competitiveness is by reducing domestic wages in dollars by a real depreciation. But the real wage cut also generates, at least in the short run, increased unemployment as the spendable income of workers is cut.

Adjustment through a gain in competitiveness thus takes a toll in terms of employment, reducing real wages and domestic demand. The increase in employment in the tradable-goods sector that should compensate is often very weak and slow. The traded-goods sector thus adopts a wait-and-see attitude, which makes real depreciation a highly precarious policy tool.*

The systemwide adjustment to forced debt service creates still another problem. Since most debtor countries have had much the same policies—overspending in the early 1980s and forced debt service now—they all resorted to real depreciation to enhance their competitiveness. But that means they cut their wages relative to one another and not only relative

---

* For examples of how individual countries handled adjustments, see the Appendix to this chapter, which examines the difficulties faced by Mexico, Brazil, the Philippines, Nigeria, and Chile.

to those of the creditor countries. As a result, any individual country cutting the dollar wage, say, by 50 percent, will gain much less in terms of increased dollar revenues because all its competitors are doing much the same.

The Budget Problem

The other major problem in the adjustment process involves the domestic budget. Much of the external debt is public or publicly guaranteed. Even that part of the debt that was not, initially, public becomes a public sector debt in the aftermath of the crisis as a result of bank failures. The government thus has to service debt that was once in private hands in addition to the public debt it had been servicing by constantly borrowing new money. The problem, of course, is where to find *extra* budget revenues of 3 or 4 percent of GDP to pay the interest costs that have suddenly been added to the budget.

The governments of the debtor countries can attempt to solve the budget problem by raising taxes and public sector prices, reducing government outlays, printing money, or issuing domestic debt. Raising taxes is notoriously difficult, since most of the taxes are already levied in the form of taxes on wages rather than incomes of the upper classes. The easier solution is to raise public sector prices or to eliminate subsidies on such items as food, transportation, and housing. The elimination of subsidies is particularly cheered by creditors and international agencies, since it means moving closer to efficient resource allocation.[2] Of course, the imposition of extra taxes or the withdrawal of subsidies is inevitably inflationary. Moreover, the direct inflationary impact is magnified by indexation of wages and the need to devalue to sustain competitiveness.

Cutting spending in the public sector is another option. Given the notorious inefficiency of the public sector, the public often believes that increased efficiency rather than trimming services or raising taxes will solve the problem. The fact is, of course, that there is very little room for public sector improvements in the short term. Large-scale firing of redundant workers would create an overwhelming political problem; plant closings would do the same; and selling inefficient, overunionized firms is difficult unless potential buyers are paid to take over the liability. Perhaps the best advice would be to suggest giving away public sector firms, but the workers would probably oppose such attempts, even if the firms were to be given to them.

In many debtor countries, governments have cut or frozen public sector wages, in some cases on a very large scale. Such a move helps the budget, but it has costs. The reduction of relative wages in the public sector promotes an exodus of the wrong kind: the best, most efficient workers are the most likely to leave.

The response to forced debt service in many of the debtor countries is to increase deficits, which are financed by issuing domestic debt or simply printing money. But expanding the money supply inevitably causes high and often extreme inflation. It is no accident that Argentina and Brazil experienced extraordinary inflation rates in the aftermath of the debt crisis. Financing the deficits by incurring debt avoids the imminent inflation problem, but does not prevent excessive debt accumulation, which ultimately poses the risk of an inflationary liquidation or a repudiation.

The budget problem does not exist in a vacuum; there is an interaction between it and the foreign exchange problem. The need to devalue to gain competitiveness implies that that part of the debt serviced in national currency will increase. A given payment of, say, $1 billion now amounts to more in pesos, to a larger peso deficit, and hence to the need for increased inflationary finance. Thus the devaluation required to earn foreign exchange is a source of inflation not only directly via the increased prices of traded goods and any accompanying indexation effects but also indirectly by raising the inflation tax. In the classical hyperinflations, major movements in the exchange rate were the prelude to the outbreak of uncontrolled inflation, and there is some evidence that exactly the same is at work in the debtor countries today.[3]

The budget is also adversely affected by capital flight. To stem capital flight, which is caused by the inflationary consequences of debt service or perhaps by a tax reform, the country will have to increase real interest rates to very high levels. These high real interest rates in turn apply to the domestic debt, causing it to grow more rapidly, thereby raising future budget deficits—and probably creating instability. That in turn creates more capital flight and yet higher rates.

There is an important trade-off in the adjustment process. In order to earn foreign exchange, wages must be cut in terms of tradable goods, thus enhancing competitiveness. But to balance the budget, it is often necessary or at least recommended that subsidies for such items as food or transportation be cut, and that also means a cut in real wages. There is thus competition between two targets, a cut in the dollar wage or the "tortilla" wage. Since there is only so much one can cut, a choice must be made. Given the slowness in the trade-sector adjustments, the competitiveness adjustment should take precedence, followed by budget balancing once the resources of the economy are reallocated. Since real depreciation alone produces slack, there is little risk of overheating if the adjustment follows this pattern.

There is also a link between budget cutting and the extraordinary cut in investment in Latin America; when it comes to government spending, the easiest cuts to make are unfortunately in the investment area. Postponing investment and maintenance is much easier than firing workers. The impact on aggregate investment is so large because the public sector, via public sector enterprises, accounts for a large part of total Latin American investment. It is obvious that governments, failing to recognize the distinction between the public sector's current and capital accounts, have chosen an ineffective means of adjustment.

What Are the Results of Adjustment?

How well individual countries handled their adjustment problems depended both on their governments' abilities and on the external conditions favoring or hindering adjustment. But there are some common characteristics of the adjustment process in all highly indebted countries. One is a decline in per capita income (see Table 3-1).

Table 3-1
Some Problem Debtors

Country	Debt per Capita	Interest/ GDP Ratio	Cumulative per Capita Consumption Change % 1980–87
Argentina	1662	7.9	– 8.4
Bolivia	662	10.0	– 36.4
Brazil	791	5.8	7.7
Chile	1740	12.9	– 15.4
Colombia	395	3.3	1.4
Costa Rica	1615	9.3	– 9.8
Mexico	1261	6.3	– 18.9
Nigeria	203	1.6	– 45.5
Peru	680	10.8	– 1.4
Philippines	456	6.2	– 7.0
Venezuela	2000	8.1	– 32.2

Source: World Bank, World Debt Tables, 1987, IMF, World Tables, 1987, and World Economic Outlook, 1987.

Table 3-2
Latin America's Debt Service and Investment
(percentage of GDP)

	1978–82	*1983–88*	*Change*
Gross Investment	24.3	19.1	– 5.2
External/Noninterest Surplus	– 0.6	4.5	5.1

Source: IMF, *World Economic Outlook,* 1988.

The other common characteristic of the adjustment process is that a significant part of the interest bill has to be, in fact, paid by turning trade balances into surpluses, primarily through cuts in investment. And since cuts in investment cause a dramatic deterioration in medium-term growth, the debt problem remains unsolved (see Table 3-2). What happens is that the improvement in the external balance, which provides the foreign exchange that is used to service debts, ends up roughly equal, and of opposite sign, to the change in investment. Thus the Latin American nations—and other debtors such as Nigeria and the Philippines—are servicing their external debt by indefinitely postponing essential investment. Overall, *net* investment is barely positive, and in some countries (for example, Argentina) it has been negative for several years. Given the high growth rates of the population, low or zero rates of net investment imply a growing disparity between capital requirements for sustained growth and actual capital in place.

All of these difficulties in adjustment help explain why the improvement in creditworthiness that the creditors expected—and which would have brought a return to voluntary lending—has not taken place. In fact, by the benchmark ratios of debt to GDP and debts to exports—creditworthiness has deteriorated since 1982.[4] Thus, not only have the creditors' hopes for adjustment not been met, but by these measures creditworthiness has deteriorated since 1982, creating even more uneasiness among creditors.

Appendix

The debtor countries each experienced a number of adjustment problems. A few cases have been chosen to demonstrate the difficulties.

Mexico. Events in Mexico provide a striking illustration of issues involved in adjustment. The least noted fact, apparent in Table 3A-1, is the dramatic shift in the budget over the past three years. The primary or *noninterest* budget has improved by 6.5 percent of GDP, showing now a solid surplus. The surplus is all the more impressive in view of the sharp oil price decline in 1986. This improvement in the noninterest budget was devoted to financing the growing interest burden on domestic and foreign debt. The *noninterest* budget has improved by more than 7 percent of GNP. From a deficit of nearly 8 percent of GDP in 1982, the noninterest balance has shifted to an estimated surplus of 4.9 percent in 1987. The improvement is all the more impressive in view of the large decline in oil revenue in 1986. Note that the improvement in the noninterest budget went to finance increased interest payments on the domestic and foreign debt.

The total budget suffered a deficit of nearly 16 percent of GDP. The increase in interest payments largely reflected inflation. Inflation and the accompanying exchange depreciation raised the nominal interest rates required to make Mexicans hold the depreciating assets. These interest rates in turn translated into a large interest bill in the budget. If by some miracle, inflation were to disappear, the budget would be nearly balanced. There is a budget deficit because there is inflation, and not the reverse.

Table 3A-2 presents details on the Mexican macroeconomic situation. In addition to the cut in public sector investment, the table shows that total investment declined dramatically, leaving little net investment.

Table 3A-1
Mexico's Fiscal Performance
(percentage of GDP)

	1980–84	*1985*	*1986*	*1987*
Budget Deficit	12.2	10.0	16.0	15.8
Primary	2.0	– 4.5	– 2.2	– 4.9
Operational	4.1	1.1	1.8	– 1.2
Public Investment	9.5	6.0	5.2	5.1

Source: R. Dornbusch, "Mexico: Stabilization, Debt and Growth," *Economic Policy,* October 1988.
Note: The primary deficit refers to the budget excluding all interest payments. The operational budget deficit includes interest payments reduced by the inflationary erosion of debt.

Consider next Mexico's international current account. There is a striking reversal of the deficits prior to the crisis to surpluses afterward. In 1983-84, the surpluses were enough to help finance capital flight and also meet the interest payments. In 1985 all of the interest was paid out of surpluses and by attracting a reflow of private capital via very high interest rates. But with the oil price decline the external financing problem returned, forcing a decision to allow further real depreciation or an alteration of the terms of debt service.

The real exchange rate and the real wage dropped dramatically in the past few years. Real wages today are 40 percent below their 1980 levels, and external competitiveness has improved by 40 percent. These are extraordinary adjustments for any country to make. Employment is not so cheerful a story. The labor force is growing at 3.5 percent per year, but employment, after an initial decline, has been stagnant over the past four years. The informal sector and migration to the United States were the main shock absorbers in employment.

Thus unemployment is increasing and with it social conflict. The lack of employment growth, even after so extreme a real depreciation of the currency, is a major concern, for it suggests that depreciation works for quite a while primarily by reducing incomes and very little by promoting exports or cutting imports. It took until 1986 for there to be signs of significant manufactures export growth. The early effects of adjustment on trade were disappointing. But recently Mexico has shown a strong

Table 3A-2
Mexico: Macroeconomic Indicators
(percent)

	1983	1984	1985	1986	1987
Per Capita Growth	– 6.2	1.4	0.6	– 6.0	– 0.6
Inflation	102.0	65.4	57.7	86.2	131.8
Investment/GDP	16.0	16.3	16.9	15.5	15.3
Real Wage (Index 1982 = 100)	77	72	73	71	68
Current Account/GDP	– 5.8	– 5.6	– 4.3	– 1.0	3.1
External Interest/GDP	7.5	7.1	7.0	6.0	5.8
Export/Price of Oil ($US/barrel)	26.4	26.8	25.4	11.9	16.0

Source: Dornbusch, "External Debt, Budget Deficits, and Disequilibrium Exchange Rates."

increase in nonoil export growth. Unfortunately, it has turned out to be a mixed blessing, with more than one hundred countervailing duty cases filed by the United States arising from the increase.

In early 1988, Mexico capitalized on the fiscal adjustment and undertook a comprehensive incomes policy program to bring down inflation. As a result of this policy, inflation came down from an annual rate of more than 400 percent in January to less than 20 percent by the end of the year. But by then a renewed collapse of oil prices and delays in dismantling the incomes policy put in question the continued success of the program.

Brazil. Like Mexico, Brazil began adjustment with a large decline in per capita income and with a sharp acceleration of inflation. The higher inflation was due largely to the real depreciation required to generate a noninterest surplus. Because wages were indexed, exchange depreciation brought still more increases in inflation. The higher inflation in turn shows up in a sharply larger budget deficit.

Table 3A-3 shows that the noninterest external balance improved sharply, as is seen in the shift of resource transfers from –1.4 percent of GDP in 1982 to a 5 percent level in 1984-85. Unlike the case of Mexico, the budget balance did not improve sharply, which stimulated growth and recovery but brought a deterioration in financial conditions.

The difference between Mexico and Brazil, in 1985-86, is both oil and macroeconomics. Lower oil prices in Brazil's case more than compensated for the adverse conditions of the domestic boom on the external balance. But the external balance is certainly also reinforced by the import substitution and export capacity expansion made possible by the

Table 3A-3
Brazil: Macroeconomic Indicators
(percent)

	1983	1984	1985	1986	1987
Inflation	142.0	197.0	227.0	142.0	225.0
Per Capita Growth	– 5.5	2.3	6.1	5.9	0.8
Operational Deficit	3.0	2.7	4.3	3.5	5.5
Resource Transfer	2.4	5.6	5.1	2.5	3.1

Source: Banco Central do Brasil, *Brazil Economic Program,* various issues.

investments of the early 1970s that came on line just in time to help service the debt.

By 1988, Brazil's economic situation was dominated by a relapse into near hyperinflation conditions. Inflation rates of more than 1,000 percent per year stopped growth and turned the economy increasingly into chaos. Pervasive corruption, declining tax morality, and a poorly conceived debt strategy severely deteriorated the prospects for economic and even political stability.

The Philippines. The example of the Philippines demonstrates the use of straightforward recession, via extraordinarily high real interest rates, as the means of adjusting. Budget cutting has reinforced the impact of tight money. The immediate effect, both in the private and public sectors, has been a sharp decline in investment (see Table 3A-4). This process, under way since 1984, has reduced per capita income by 15 percent. The current account thus improved, in spite of a real appreciation.

By 1986, lower oil prices and a major depreciation of the currency had helped turn the current account toward an actual surplus of more than 3 percent of GNP. But that was a year when per capita income was still declining. The immediate question is what happens when a policy of 6 percent growth, to which the government is committed, is implemented. Either more of the external interest is borrowed, thus providing financing for current account deficits, or a balance-of-payments crisis

Table 3A-4
Philippines: Macroeconomic Indicators
(percent)

	1975–82	1983	1984	1985	1986	1987
Per Capita Growth	2.9	– 1.5	– 7.5	2.9	– 10.1	2.7
Inflation	11.8	10.2	50.3	23.1	0.8	3.8
Investment [c]	30.0	27.1	17.4	14.3	13.2	14.6
Resource Transfer [c]	– 5.8[a]	– 6.8	– 0.6	2.8	5.9	– 0.2
Budget Deficit [c]	3.2[a]	1.9	1.8	1.8	5.0	2.8
Terms of Trade [b]	101.0	92.4	96.2	92.6	80.1	87.0

Source: IMF and World Bank.
[a] 1980–82   [b] Index 1980 = 100   [c] % of GDP

is inevitable. The Philippines is an example of a debt problem that is far from solved.

Nigeria. In Nigeria the debt problem has been severely aggravated by mismanagement in the early 1980s and by the sharp decline of oil prices in 1985-86. Per capita income has declined 30 percent over the period.

Working under a strict IMF program, the country is now trying to restore productive activity in the nonoil traditional export sector. The exchange rate, once distorted by the use of licenses and black markets, has been unified, which has helped restore incentives to the economy.

While on the exchange rate side adjustment has been important, and has already brought an improved export performance for traditional goods, the dramatic decline in investment is a barrier to economic growth (see Table 3A-5). Increased borrowing to finance both the decline in oil prices and the interest bill would mean increasing debt burdens, and that can only be justified if significantly higher oil prices are expected.

Chile. The level of per capita consumption in Chile today is the same as it was in 1960. There are two reasons. The first is the sharp deterioration in the terms of trade, especially as a result of the massive decline in copper prices. Copper in 1987 commanded half the real price it did in 1970 when copper accounted for nearly 30 percent of exports. Increased oil prices in the late 1970s and the decline in real agricultural prices made things worse.

The other reason for the poor growth performance was the mismanagement of the exchange rate in 1978-82, which left Chile with an unparal-

Table 3A-5
Nigeria: Macroeconomic Indicators
(percent)

	1983	1984	1985	1986	1987
Per Capita Growth	– 9.6	– 8.5	2.0	0.0	– 6.7
Inflation	23.2	39.6	5.5	5.5	10.2
Budget Deficit	9.6	4.2	2.6	3.3	10.1
Investment	16.8	12.3	9.6	n.a.	n.a.
Resource Transfer	4.1	2.1	4.1	– 1.8	5.2

n.a. = not available.
Source: IMF and World Bank.

leled burden. Chile's per capita debt is higher than that of any other country, and interest payments are an extraordinary 12 percent of GDP. This compares with 5 to 6 percent in Mexico or Brazil.

Since the deep recession of 1982-83, Chile has enjoyed some growth in per capita income (see Table 3A-6), but the level, of course, is still far below that of 1980. Despite the decline in the terms of trade, the noninterest current account has run a surplus of more than 5 percent of GDP. This was possible because of a very substantial real depreciation.

Chile is certainly one of the debtor countries least likely to become solvent. Because the decline in per capita income is sustained by a repressive regime, if a democratic government comes to power it will be faced with demands for a restoration of living standards and social benefits, and above all, for an increase in employment. To meet the challenge of providing higher living standards, and at the same time restore investment, the external debt will have to be written down—declared a political debt negotiated between the Pinochet government and the creditor banks that sustained him in power. It is hard to believe that such a move would face much opposition in Western democracies.

Table 3A-6
Chile: Macroeconomic Indicators
(percent)

	1982	1983	1984	1985	1986	1987
Per Capita Growth	- 14.5	- 2.2	4.3	0.7	3.2	3.4
Inflation	21.0	24.0	23.0	26.0	17.0	21.5
Investment	14.6	12.0	12.3	14.2	14.2	15.2
Resource Transfers	- 2.0	2.7	- 0.7	3.2	4.2	3.2
Terms of Trade	76.0	84.0	78.0	73.0	86.0	91.0
Debt/GDP	71.3	92.1	104.0	126.5	123.0	112.0

Source: World Bank and Economic Commission for Latin America.

Chapter 4
Bank Exposure and the Quality of Debts

One of the major issues in the debt crisis is the probable effect of outright repudiation or a write-down of debts. At the end of 1987, the total exposure of U.S. banks to the heavily indebted developing countries was less than $100 billion, approximately 80 percent of bank capital. Since there is little or no chance of all these debtors repudiating all of their debts simultaneously, the picture is far more favorable than public discussion would indicate. And even if the major debtors—all of Latin America, Nigeria, the Philippines, Morocco, and Yugoslavia—repudiated their debts at the same time, the equity of U.S. bank stockholders would not be completely wiped out—and depositors would not be hurt at all.

That at any rate is the picture for all U.S. banks; the situation changes when banks are grouped for size (see Table 4-1). The nine major banks account for 74 percent of the loans, the next thirteen largest for another 20 percent. In addition, the loans are not spread out evenly across all countries: Brazil, Mexico, Argentina, and the Philippines account for more than half of capital.

It is also important to remember that Latin America's debt is not held only by U.S. banks. The Bank for International Settlements reports a Latin American debt of $160 billion in 1985, only half of which is owed to U.S. banks. For the remaining problem debtors, the BIS total is $37 billion, only a third of which is owed U.S. banks.[1]

There are also important differences in exposure between European and U.S. banks. During the period of dollar appreciation, European banks

Table 4-1
U.S. Bank Exposure to Problem Debtors, March 1988

	$ Billion	Percentage of Capital
9 Money Center Banks	52.2	99.6
13 Other Large Banks	13.8	58.3
All Other Banks	11.3	20.5

Source: Federal Financial Institutions Examination Council.
Note: Problem debtors are defined as Latin America, including Venezuela, plus Nigeria, the Philippines, Ivory Coast, and Morocco.

were forced to increase their reserves against dollar loans. Furthermore, these loan provisions were facilitated by tax advantages. In addition, since 1985 the dollar has depreciated significantly, which has further increased European loan-loss reserves relative to their claims. Thus, unlike U.S. banks, European banks are said to have, in some instances, been able to fully cover problem debts.

To judge the size of these debts and the resulting vulnerability of banks it is helpful to remember that in June 1987 U.S. banks had capital (including loan-loss reserves) of $124.4 billion. The nine large money-center banks had capital equal to $49.24 billion. The reserve buildup is still under way. As a result, the exposure, even of large banks, has been significantly reduced. In 1985, the nine large money-center banks had an exposure of near 150 percent of their capital. Today the ratio of problem-debtor loans has fallen already below 100 percent of capital, and that ratio is steadily declining as a result of reserve provision, write-offs, and loan sales.

The Quality of Banks and Debts

From the nineteenth century until World War II, developing-country debt usually was in the form of bonds traded on organized markets and widely held by the public. The postwar debt, by contrast, is owed to official institutions and commercial banks. Since few of the claims on debtor countries take the form of bonds, there are no good price quotations to use to measure the quality of debts. But for some time, bank claims on various debtors have been swapped or sold outright between banks—and now some are even sold to nonbanks. This market has become central to discussions of debt-equity swaps. In these transactions, purchase of discounted debt is the starting point for foreign investment in a debtor country.

Table 4-2 shows the average of the bid and offer price in the so-called swap market. Even though all debts are not actively traded, the prices provide some indication of market value.

There are large differences in discounts between countries. The debts of Peru and Nigeria have a very low valuation. Bolivian debt (not shown in the table) trades at a price of only 10 cents (a discount of 90 percent), while Colombia, a country that has so far paid all interest punctually, still has a discount of more than 10 percent. The price of the debts of Mexico and Venezuela has declined, which can be attributed to the oil price decline. But Mexico's low price seems to ignore the extraordinary domestic adjustments that have been made over the past year. Thus it is difficult to see precisely how differences in a country's ability and willingness to service the debt translate into discounts, but as Table 4-3 indicates, discounts do seem to shift over time.

Table 4-2
Some Problem Debts

Country	Total Debt $ billion	Debt to U.S. Banks		Price * (Cents/$)	
		All Banks $ billion	9 Banks $ billion	3/87	10/88
Argentina	50.8	8.4	6.0	65.0	22.4
Brazil	107.3	22.2	15.2	66.0	46.3
Chile	21.0	6.5	4.1	68.0	58.4
Colombia	11.3	2.2	1.6	86.5	66.2
Mexico	99.0	24.2	13.5	57.5	47.2
Nigeria	19.3	0.9	0.7	37.0	24.0
Peru	13.4	1.5	0.8	19.0	6.0
Philippines	24.8	5.1	3.7	70.0	51.8
Uruguay	3.6	0.9	0.7	72.0	60.5
Venezuela	33.6	9.7	6.9	75.0	46.5

Source: Federal Reserve, World Bank, and dealer information.
* Average price in cents-per-dollar debt.

Table 4-3
Prices in the Secondary Market for Bank Loans
(Cents-per-Dollar Face Value)

	7/85	7/86	1/87	7/87	10/88
Argentina	60	63	62	47	22
Brazil	75	73	74	57	46
Mexico	80	56	54	54	47
Peru	45	18	16	11	6
Philippines	n.a.	n.a.	72	68	52
Venezuela	81	75	77	69	47

n.a. = not available.
Source: Shearson, Lehman Brothers and Salomon Brothers Inc.

The average price of the debts of the countries covered in Table 4-3 is now less than 50 cents per dollar, down over the past two years. The overall picture of discounts of 50 percent and more suggests that these are problem debts, and that therefore the prospect of a return to voluntary lending is remote.

But the story is more complicated than that. Consider the case of Uruguay. The country's debt stands at a discount of 40 percent, suggesting that repayment of the debt is problematic. Yet, in the fall of 1986, Uruguay issued a long-term public bond at a rate not far above the rate on U.S. Treasury notes, and Colombia has floated a $50 million public bond in Luxembourg. Perhaps the large discounts in the swap market reflect a market that is so narrow that the illiquidity of banks brings down the prices. But would Colombia have borrowed $500 million rather than only $50 million, and at what rate, if this were not the case? This question is critical in evaluating the possibility of voluntary lending. Recently, Colombia sought to secure a rollover of $1.5 billion in principal that is maturing over the next three years. Commercial banks seemed reluctant to reschedule, taking the position that Colombia should go to the bond market, use debt-equity swaps and World Bank cofinancing—anything but commercial bank loans. What this suggests, in the clearest terms, is that commercial banks are retreating from Latin America, even in the case of the least troubled debtors.

Chapter 5
Solutions to the Debt Problem: General Issues and the Baker Plan

A great many proposals for solving the debt crisis have been put forth since 1982. They range from cosmetic tinkering to outright default or repudiation of debt. Some proposals involve an increased role for creditor governments and their taxpayers, others make a point of removing governments from the debt collection process. In order to assess the advantages and disadvantages of the major proposals, it is necessary to know exactly what problems they would have to solve.

First, the transfer of real resources must be reversed, and the flow of development capital to the debtor countries must resume. The noninterest surpluses, which the debtor countries are now using to service debt, must again be turned into deficits to provide new resources to supplement domestic saving in financing growth.

As long as the existing debt is judged to be of poor quality, commercial banks will be reluctant to put up new money to finance even the cost of interest on that debt. They will not lend over and above the interest bill. Moreover, since the old debt clearly has first claim on the debtor countries' resources, it is impossible to attract new lenders or investors. The existing debt also places a burden on economic growth, making these countries even less attractive to foreign investors, who also fear a political backlash. Thus, until the problem of old debts is resolved one way or another, fresh capital will be very hard to find.

Second, even though the market appraises the debts of problem debtors at, on average, less than 50 cents (indicating the possibility that some of these debts will never be repaid), debtor countries do not benefit from these implicit write-offs. When a small bank takes a loss, selling off a claim on, say, Bolivia, at 10 cents on the dollar, the buyer acquires a claim that he can try to collect to the full value. The debtor country thus bears the full burden of trying to service that debt. The burden, even if nothing is paid, takes the form of uncertainty—and uncertainty has an adverse effect on a country's economy. By contrast, if the banks were to write down the loans, it would reduce the probability of default, thereby improving the overall debt-service climate.

There are other problems: the ability of the commercial banks to take the losses involved in any debt consolidation and the difficulty posed by the regulatory environment. These issues are important because of the divergent interests of large and small banks, and the differences between U.S. and foreign banks. In addition, U.S. regulations are ambiguous about the consequences of debt consolidation, that is, the renegotiation of loans involving substantial changes in terms. There is little doubt that if consolidation were forced on the banks the costs to them would be minimized through favorable tax treatment—the losses would be spread out over an extended period of time. But regulations make it very expensive for banks to decide to consolidate. This may be because the regulatory authorities want to discourage any eagerness on the part of creditors to give in to consolidation. Of course, this position also stands in the way of reasonable settlements for some claims, which as a consequence may deteriorate in value.

Finally, there is the problem creditor countries have in reconciling the conflicting interests of commercial banks, manufacturers, and foreign policy. Maintaining the stability and profitability of the banking system is an important objective. But it may compete with other objectives—in the case of the United States, for example, our interest in stable democratic governments on our borders or in the health of our own manufacturing sector.

These are the major problems that will have to be dealt with by any proposal. But those who put forth proposals for solving the debt problem must also decide whether or not creditor governments should be involved and whether or not consolidation should be an objective.

There is a fundamental difference between those who argue that governments should completely withdraw from the debt collection process and those who see a role for government or even want to see the role of government expanded. The former position is held by the country's most distinguished conservative economists.[1] At the other end of the spectrum are plans that involve a much increased, though also modified, government involvement. Many different proposals based on this approach[2] have been put forth by members of Congress and the investment banking community.[3]

Both groups recognize that debt consolidation is, in some instances, necessary if the debt problem is to be solved. That puts them in opposition to the Baker Plan, which has as its premise that debts can and should be kept fully alive and productive in terms of interest. Although the banking community initially endorsed the Baker Plan, enthusiasm has been withering in the aftermath of the 1986 Mexican settlement. Morgan Guaranty has come out most strongly on this point:

> . . . industrial country governments should recognize that the 50-50 split between private and official funds typical of many past new money packages for the debtor countries may not be a workable norm for the future, nor is indefinite reliance on "involuntary lending" by banks. Realism demands an increased share of new money be furnished by official sources during the next several years.[4]

Multilateral institutions have, by and large, taken their cue from the U.S. government, and the International Monetary Fund has taken the initiative in organizing involuntary lending.[5]

Most debt proposals focus on some form of consolidation along with substantial government intervention. To place the various proposals that have recently been suggested in their proper perspective, it is important to examine the Baker Plan first.

The Baker Plan

In fall 1985, U.S. Treasury Secretary James Baker proposed a broad-ranging and ambitious plan for dealing with the debt crisis. Recognizing that the debt problem would not soon disappear, he put forward a plan that called for servicing and ultimately repaying the debt. To meet those objectives would take:

- continued involvement by commercial banks, who were asked to contribute the "new money" needed for the rescheduling of debt;
- sharply increased participation and lending by multilateral institutions, especially the World Bank;
- focus on debtor-country adjustment, not only by belt-tightening of the 1982-84 variety, but also by a positive focus on free enterprise

and supply-side economics, direct investment, and a return of capital flight;
• sustained world economic growth and lower interest rates to encourage adjustment by the debtor countries.

The Baker Plan clearly was more a philosophical approach to the debt problem than a blueprint for gradually eliminating it. Because the plan was so general, there was, of course, little to disagree with, and because it had so few specifics, aside from increased lending by multilateral agencies, there was very little for anyone to endorse. Despite its good intentions, the Baker Plan had little effect. The economic and political problems in the debtor countries require far more specific help.

Free Enterprise and Efficiency in Government

Any serious discussion of solutions to the debt problem must start by rejecting the conventional wisdom that debtor countries can overcome their predicament by pulling up their socks, making their public sectors more efficient, privatizing state enterprises, and removing obstacles to foreign direct investment. There is no reason to believe that these measures would make a significant difference to the debt problem over the next few years. Even their importance as short-term remedies has been exaggerated, perhaps to focus attention on solutions to the debt problem that do not place greater burdens on the creditors.

It is also important to recognize that many of the proposed reforms create political problems. For example, many complain that Argentina and Mexico have done very little or nothing to make their public enterprises more efficient. Why has Mexico still not closed down the sugar and steel industries? Why does Pemex in Mexico or YPF in Argentina remain in the public sector rather than being sold?

While inefficiency in the public sector is wasteful, that waste also represents the standard of living of those who hold jobs in these enterprises. Eliminating waste means cutting the living standards of often highly organized groups. A weak government waits until there is enough support generated by successful stabilization to move to the more difficult and more politicized problem areas. Both Argentina and Mexico appear to have had some success with this strategy. If their restructuring had not been gradual, their governments might well have encountered more organized resistance, which would have impaired the entire adjustment effort.

More important, much of the advice from creditor countries and international agencies has focused exclusively on spending cuts and increased efficiency, ignoring the disastrously low taxes collected in debtor countries such as Argentina and Brazil. It is critical that a more reasonable system of taxation be put in place in order to ensure the funds for economic development.

Direct Investment and the Return of Capital Flight

The Baker Plan called for the debtor countries to create an environment that would encourage foreign investment and bring about a repatriation of private capital. But direct investment has never accounted for more than about 10 percent of total capital flows to the debtor countries (see Table 5-1), and much of that amount probably represents a reinvestment of earnings rather than an addition to foreign exchange resources.

Investment flows may be small because the investment climate is so hostile. An emphasis on equity finance instead of borrowing might have served the debtor countries much better, but nationalist arguments precluded such a course, landing the debtors in a much more serious state of dependence than massive foreign control of equity could ever have done. That being said, it is doubtful that foreign direct investment is likely to play a quantitatively significant role at this point. Even doubling the rate of direct investment would contribute only a small share of the resources needed for debt service. There is, though, a qualitative argument in favor of increased direct foreign investment. It looks good from a business point of view and may influence skeptical domestic investors to put their money in the domestic market.

Much the same can be said about the repatriation of capital. There has been a good deal of wishful thinking about the $100 billion or more

Table 5-1
Financing of Current Account Deficits: Fifteen Debtors
($ billion, annual average)

	1980–82	1983–87
Borrowing	50.2	12.9
Nondebt Flows	6.8	4.8

Source: International Monetary Fund.

of Latin assets that have fled from their home countries to escape the effects of political instability or to evade taxation. Although the precise figures for capital flight are not known, there is no question that it took place on an extraordinary scale in the case of Argentina, Mexico, and Venezuela. Many believe that reversing this capital flight, especially in the case of Mexico or Argentina, would make it possible to pay off the entire external debt, most of which went to finance that capital flight.[6]

But it is difficult to accept the idea that the return of private capital could be the solution to the debt problem, or at least an important part of the solution. There is little historical precedent for a major reflow. And, if it is to happen, it is likely that it will happen only when the residents of the debtor countries believe that the major problems have been solved; it will not be part of the solution. The only exception to this rule is when a nation follows a monetary policy that is so tight that high interest rates and economic necessity cause a return of capital. But that, of course, is counterproductive from a business point of view.

It is often argued that, if countries would adopt policies that enabled them to guarantee savers stable positive real rates of interest, the capital flight problem would vanish. But that argument does not hold up. First, during adjustment, devaluation is unavoidable. If governments were to compensate savers for the loss they would have avoided by holding dollar assets, the burden on the budget would be intolerable, creating financial and, possibly, political instability. Second, high, positive real interest rates pose a serious risk to public finance; when the public debt carries high real rates, domestic debt increases rapidly—and again the result is instability. Third, it is a very bad habit to raise the return on paper assets above the prospective return on real capital. That is poor supply-side economics, and it eventually erodes the tax base and causes the financial system to deteriorate.

There are two examples of significant reflows of capital: Mexico in 1985-87 and Turkey. In each case, the authorities used exceptionally high real interest rates to repatriate capital. For more than a year, Mexico financed interest payments on the foreign debt by net capital inflows. Interest rates were set so high that firms could not borrow in the home market and had to repatriate capital simply to stay in business.

In Turkey, the government sought to attract lending from Turkish workers in West Germany.[7] The government arranged with Germany's Dresdner Bank to create a special D-Mark-denominated deposit for Turkish workers, the proceeds of which would be available for the Turkish government. The deposit carried a rate more than three percentage points above LIBOR. These deposits have become an important source of external finance, amounting to more than 20 percent of current external liabilities. The attraction of these deposits (guaranteed by a German bank in D-Marks) is that they pay far more than the deposit rates available in the Euromarket.

It is not clear how the Turkish government can pay such high rates, except temporarily. Perhaps the strategy is to demonstrate a reduced dependence on involuntary bank lending as an intermediate stage before attempting a full-fledged return to the world capital market. Because of the extraordinarily high rates paid and the short-term nature of the deposits, this scheme will not solve the debt problem, but it might be interesting for the Mexican government to look into the experience to see whether it could be adopted for Mexican workers in the United States.[8]

The United States is, to some extent, responsible for the capital flight problem. In an effort to fund the U.S. deficits at low cost, the Reagan administration eliminated the withholding tax on nonresidents' investments—and other countries followed suit. The only purpose one can imagine for this policy is to persuade foreigners to use the U.S. financial system as a tax haven. To invest in Mexico, anyone paying taxes there would need to earn quite a few extra percentage points interest and be willing to accept risks, such as the possibility of depreciation of the peso.

There is much talk about the problems of banks putting new money into the debtor countries only to see it leave; of every extra dollar of new money conceded by creditors, 70 cents are said to leave in capital flight. But the fact is that the large commercial banks in the United States are the chief vehicles for and beneficiaries of the capital flight. Capital flight, by placing an even more serious adjustment burden on workers in the debtor countries, increases the risk that the debt crisis will cause political problems.

Debt-Equity Swaps

For creditors seeking new ways to liquidate the massive foreign debts they have in their portfolios, debt-equity swaps offer an attractive partial solution—and they are very much in the spirit of the Baker Plan.[9] Their apparent merit is that they allow banks to sell off loans without a massive decline in loan prices, and at the same time, they enable debtors to reduce their external debt while pulling in foreign investment.

Debt-equity swaps between private firms and their commercial bank creditors (without government intervention or subsidies) are entirely appropriate. Similarly, there cannot be any objection to direct foreign investment. On the contrary, there should have been more in the past, and the more there is in the future, the better. The only objections are to the use of an already strained government budget to subsidize foreign direct investment and bank divestment.

The basic difficulty is that debt-equity swaps amount to a budget subsidy by debtor countries that will let banks get out and foreign investors get in. The mechanics go like this: First Regional Bank sells Brazilian government bonds at a discount to Dreams, Inc., a U.S. firm specializing in services. Dreams, Inc., presents the debt to the Banco Central do Brasil to be paid off in cruzados. The proceeds are used for the purchase of a Brazilian firm. It seems that everybody gains: the bank has found a way of selling some of its illiquid portfolio without depressing the secondhand market; the investing firm gains the advantage of buying cruzados at a discount; and Brazil gains because it can pay the foreign debt in local currency rather than in dollars. Moreover, much needed investment takes place.

So why are the debtor governments so reluctant to engage in debt-equity swaps? Their first objection is that they will have to finance the repurchase of debt from the foreign investor. They cannot simply print local money to pay. In fact, the government will issue domestic debt and use the proceeds to buy back its foreign debt as it is presented by the foreign investor. The result will be a reduced external debt but a matching increase in domestic debt. The country owns less of its capital stock, since the foreign investor will have bought some and in return has redeemed some of its external debt.

Debt-equity swaps have an undesirable effect on the budget because the reduced interest payments on external debts are offset by increased domestic debt service. There is a net reduction in interest if the debtor country can appropriate most of the discount at which the external debt is traded and if the domestic rates (in dollars) are not too high relative to the cost of servicing the external debt. The net result is, however, likely to be an increase in debt service because real interest rates in debtor countries are exceptionally high.

On the balance-of-payments side, swaps might seem to be workable: foreign debt is reduced, and as a result, burdensome interest payments come down. But the reduced external interest payments are matched, at least potentially, by increased remittances of dividends or profits of the new foreign owners of the national capital stock. Hence, on the payments side, the swaps also fail to do much good. The country becomes less liquid, since it is much easier to control the service of bank debt than the remittances of multinationals. In the extreme, of course, debt-equity swaps can lend themselves to outright abuse in the form of "round-tripping," where a firm uses the right to remit profits at the official exchange rate and brings the money back into the country via a debt-equity swap. The outflow of remittances from Brazil in 1986 is a case in point.

Debt-equity swaps are primarily a balance-sheet operation, not a means of drawing in extra investment. It can be argued that the government could target deals to make them less a transaction in existing assets and instead direct them to new, extra investment. More likely, financial intermediaries will look for firms, domestic or foreign, that are already planning to invest in the country and approach them with a new kind of financing package involving debt-equity swaps, which because of an implicit subsidy by the government turn out to be less costly than other sources of finance. Thus, although the debt-equity swaps will finance investment, they do so at the budget cost of a subsidy, and the investment would have taken place anyway.

The Mexican experience has been that direct foreign investment fell virtually one-for-one with the amount of debt-equity swaps, suggesting that debt-equity swaps just financed investment that would have taken place anyway. The implication for the government is that, in addition to budget issues, there is a reduced foreign exchange inflow and hence reduced resources for import liberalization or for maintaining the exchange rate in the face of speculative capital outflows.

Debt-equity swaps are supposed to do two things: allow banks to get out of developing-country debts, even though the debtor countries are unable to pay, and make fresh resources available to the debtors' economies. A free, unregulated market would do both. It would allow the banks to mark down their shaky loans enough to sell them to the nonbank public, and it would enable the debtor countries to set up investment funds through which nonresidents could invest in the private economy. This is what "securitization" is all about. As a result, old, bad debts would stop being a mortgage on new investment. Under such a system, the bad debts are distributed more widely (though at a loss to stockholders of the banks), and the debtor countries gain extra resources that can be used to expand investment or to buy back debt. This would be the market solution. Debt-equity swaps, by contrast, are a way of nationalizing the transaction. They provide budget subsidies by debtor countries for stockholders of commercial banks rather than subsidizing extra investment.

But balance-sheet tricks are not a substitute for gaining extra real resources for investment. Improved government budgets in the debtor countries, increased efficiency in their public sector, and net resource transfers from abroad are the only way for investment and growth to resume. Debtor countries should open the doors to foreign direct investment, but there is no justification for subsidizing that investment.

IMF estimates suggest that in the period from 1984 to 1987 nearly $10 billion of official debt conversions took place. In 1988 these numbers increased vastly as a result of a Brazilian decision to buy back at auction more than $3 billion while at the same time condoning a wave of "informal" debt conversions by state enterprises. But the enthusiasm for massive debt conversion was shortlived because of the explosive inflationary effect of the resulting money creation. By late 1988, informal conversions were suspended, and even the auction process came under review.

The World Macroeconomy. An important premise of the Baker Plan was that steady growth in the industrial countries and moderate interest rates would help solve the debt problem. How valid is this assumption? There is little doubt that a return of the high interest rates of 1981, for example, would lead many debtor countries to balk at further adjustment programs. If rates were to rise, they might choose to repudiate their debts, blaming their inability to pay on the policies of the creditor countries.

The world economy will be dominated over the next few years by the U.S. efforts to reduce its deficits and the reaction of Europe and Japan to the deflationary shock that will follow from those efforts. The questions that will have to be answered are: Can adjustment take place without a significant reduction in world growth? And will world real interest rates decline in the course of the adjustment?

The U.S. fiscal adjustment will mean higher taxes and a reduction in disposable income and spending for Americans, which inevitably lead to a slowdown of the U.S. economy. This will be countered by the expansionary influences from the trade-balance adjustment that is already under way as a result of the dollar's decline, which plays a key role in the adjustment.

There are two unfavorable scenarios for debtors. In the first, there is fiscal adjustment in the United States with no significant monetary accommodation, either in the United States or elsewhere. In that case world growth declines substantially, and that decline is reflected in a poorer trade performance of LDCs, lower real commodity prices, and perhaps increased protectionism.

In the second, U.S. fiscal adjustment leads, via the recession-induced decline in interest rates, to a sharp fall of the dollar on foreign markets. If the dollar depreciation proves inflationary, the Federal Reserve might well see the need to *raise* rather than lower interest rates. This worst-case scenario looks very much like 1981-82—higher interest rates and world recession—but it is a possibility that cannot be ruled out.

A third scenario would be much more favorable for the debtor countries. In this scenario, U.S. fiscal adjustment is accompanied by a world-wide reduction in interest rates at substantially unchanged exchange rates. With exchange rates unchanged, inflation is not an issue; with the reduction in interest rates, the slack created by higher taxes and/or reduced spending is absorbed by an increase in interest-sensitive spending. World growth does not decline; debtor countries enjoy a decline in interest rates and with it a reduction in debt service—and continued growth.

The Economic Commission for Latin America has prepared estimates of the impact on various Latin American countries of a two and one-half percentage point reduction in interest rates (Table 5-2). The impact of that reduction on individual debtor countries will depend both on their debt ratios and on the fraction of debt that is at floating rates.

Table 5-2
Interest Saving from a 2.5 Percentage Point Fall in Interest Rates

	$ billion	% of Goods and Services
Latin America	6.0	7.8
Mexico	2.0	10.5
Venezuela	0.5	5.7
Bolivia	0.025	3.5
Chile	0.4	9.4
Argentina	0.8	15.7
Brazil	1.7	10.3
Peru	0.14	5.1

Source: Economic Commission for Latin America.

The impact of interest rates on import availability is significant for Mexico, Argentina, and Brazil, who borrow heavily from commercial banks. For Latin America as a whole, a 2.5 percent reduction in interest rates would amount to a resource saving of nearly 8 percent of total imports, which is why the monetary policies used by the United States to correct its deficit are so important. Unfortunately, Europe and Japan have so far been unwilling to adopt policies that would reduce interest rates, while the Federal Reserve has shifted to tighter credit in an effort to prevent a further decline in the dollar. From the point of view of debtor countries, and the world economy, the current policy mix is hard to defend.

Cartel Fatigue. Under the Baker Plan, sustaining involuntary lending has been a problem. Small banks with minor loan exposure find it increasingly burdensome and unrewarding to participate in restructuring debts. They prefer selling off their claims or simply not participating in new rounds of concerted lending.

In the Mexican rescheduling, only 40 percent of the more than four hundred participating banks had agreed to sign on by early 1987, months after the agreement with the advisory group had been reached. It was March 1987 before, under the pressure of the Brazilian moratorium, the bankers actually completed the rescheduling. (The delay between the initial agreement and the final commitment was well over half a year.) In terms of the total commitment of new money, the participation of the small banks is inconsequential, which means that the debts become increasingly concentrated in the hands of the major banks, whose credit ratings slip as a result of their exposure. This means that the cost of their capital increases, and that increase is inevitably passed on to the debtors. That, in turn, makes it even more difficult for the debtor countries to keep up with their payments. Hence the obvious problem of keeping the cartel alive.

In September 1988, the managing director of the Institute of International Finance, a lobby for banks with severe exposure to problem debtors, wrote to the chairmen of the Interim and Development Committees on the occasion of the IMF-World Bank annual meeting, summarizing why there cannot be an expectation that commercial banks continue to be a source of new money in rescheduling agreements. Among the reasons, he noted insufficient profitability of lending in view of new capital requirements that raise the cost of lending to debtor countries, reduced cohesion among banks and divergent accounting and regulatory requirements, and the "chilling effect" of increased arrearages and calls for debt forgiveness. He concludes, ". . . the demand for bank financing from developing countries exceeds the capacity and willingness of banks to supply it. Moreover, banks are seeking new lines of business."

Even as bank fatigue becomes increasingly apparent, major new reschedulings are concluded. A major program for Brazil was negotiated in 1988, and a new money package for Mexico will be necessary shortly. The difficulties in putting together such programs, the strain among banks, and the pervasiveness of expensive golden handshakes and parachutes, especially in the Brazil agreement, make it unlikely that the process can continue as such for many years. Indeed, a recent bank proposal for Brazil's external financing for the next five years makes this quite apparent. The proposal envisages a *reduction* in the principal of Brazil's debt of nearly $18 billion; this is to be achieved by trade surpluses that pay all of the interest and, in combination with debt conversions, help reduce the principal.

Protectionism. The final complication is rising protectionism in the creditor countries, especially in the United States. The debt crisis increases the problems of U.S. firms that find it hard to sell in countries that have reduced spending on imports as part of their adjustment program. In addition, debtor countries are again, in response to adjustment, increasing their exports. The U.S. response has taken the form of a much more rigorous enforcement of the trade laws. While lip service is being paid to free trade, protectionist pressure is mounting.

In summary, the Baker Plan was far from problem-free. Realistically speaking, debtor countries could not resume growth and, at the same time, service debts at full value. Unless some solution is found, and many have been put forth, both the credit ratings of the creditor banks and the economies of the debtor countries will continue to deteriorate.

Chapter 6
Radical Solutions

The radical proposals for solving the debt problem fall into two categories: the conservative, which recommends a complete government withdrawal from debt collection, and the activist, which proposes that the debtor countries take unilateral action, going into indefinite arrears, either by declaring a moratorium on or a repudiation of their debts.[1] The proposals put forth by each group are extreme, but while those in the first category offer a plausible solution, those in the second cannot be recommended except under the most extraordinary circumstances.

It is virtually impossible to support repudiation under any circumstance. But there is a need for responsible unilateral action that restructures debts in such a way that a country's capacity for growth can be improved without impairing its long-run ability to honor its debt commitments. (This possibility will be looked at in Chapter 9.)

The Conservative Recommendation

The conservative position is best summarized by the resolution of the group known as the Shadow Financial Regulatory Committee:

> We oppose the Baker plan. The plan shows a lack of political discipline. The international debt problem is a problem for the banks to work out with the principal debtors. The Baker plan shifts onto the tax payers, in an indirect and roundabout way, costs arising from prospective losses that should be borne by bank owners and managers.[2]

Milton Friedman has expressed much the same opinion:

> So I think the way you solve the LDC "debt bomb" problem is to require the people who make the loans to collect them. If they can, fine, and if they can't, that's their problem.[3]

What would be the effect of a government withdrawal from the debt collection process? For example, what if the World Bank were to refuse to continue to provide extra financing in the guise of structural adjustment loans (SALs)? And what if individual governments would no longer try to force debtor countries to honor their debts?

In the absence of public financing and the arm-twisting that has accompanied it, creditors and debtors would have to strike a bargain on the terms of the debt. Debtors would be in a much stronger position because of the absence of political pressures that are sometimes overwhelming. Some countries would make agreements with their creditors on concessions: write-downs, interest rate concessions, and a grace period in exchange for some form of conditionality, especially in relation to public finance. Other countries might suffer because they were unable to effectively resist the creditor cartel. Still other countries would find that they lose the advantage of obtaining public sector money, such as World Bank funds, without gaining from the absence of political pressures.

An added attraction of the market solution is that it would allow debts to be written down because banks would no longer expect taxpayers to eventually foot the bill. But the write-down would be conditional; that is, if the country's fortunes were to revive—oil prices go up, for example—the creditors would share in the benefits. Such a market-oriented settlement would eliminate the current system in which claims are valued far below par, but are held in the hope that the taxpayer might take them over or guarantee them at par. Undoubtedly, the market solution would also allow debtor countries to make adjustments in public finance and develop investment policies designed to enhance their ability to service their debts.[4]

Allan Meltzer, a leading conservative economist, has described a plan that would give banks, as partial payment of their claims, equity in state enterprises in the debtor countries. But, he admits, debtors would be unlikely to settle without some gain:

> If the debtor countries repaid some of their loans by giving banks equity positions in national companies, the charade would end. The action would

force the banks to recognize losses, possibly very large ones. The debtor countries would insist on settling claims at less than 100 cents on the dollar of debt. Otherwise they would have no incentive to abandon the present folly of piling loan upon loan in hopes that, someday, they will not have to borrow just to pay interest.

The size of the losses that banks would have to accept could be settled only in negotiation between them and the debtors. My very rough estimate is that it might take write-offs of 20 to 30 percent of the face value of the loans if the obligations of problem countries were reduced to market value. . . .

As always, the debtors can't pay because a mistake was made. Who made the mistake is unimportant. The crucial task now is to admit the error, put it behind us, and work toward a solution that permits an increase in world trade and standards of living.[5]

The recommendation of the conservatives takes us back to the situation in the 1930s, where the government made a point that it would not collect private debts:

> . . . the making of satisfactory arrangements and protecting of American interests was [according to a White House announcement on October 20, 1933] "a task primarily for private initiative and interests. The traditional policy of the American Government has been that such loan and investment transactions were primarily private actions, to be handled by the parties directly concerned. The Government realizes a duty, within the proper limits of international law and international amity, to defend American interests abroad. However, it would not be wise for the Government to undertake directly the settlement of private debt situations."[6]

Today, the U.S. government is actively involved, with carrot and club, in seeing that debts remain collectible. The government took this position as a spontaneous reaction to the Mexican liquidity crisis in 1982, perhaps because of the vulnerability of the commercial banking system. In addition, the governments of the industrial countries were already involved through their participation in the multilateral organizations, especially the World Bank and the IMF, who are responsible for coordinating rescue packages and avoiding financial crises.

Many observers might say that no questions should be raised about the role of governments in this context; it seems desirable for governments to avoid financial crises. The conservatives counter by pointing out that the ultimate crisis is made worse and more crisis situations are encouraged when governments are seen to collect bad debts as a matter of policy. In such situations, bad loans are encouraged, and the taxpayer puts up the interest.

The conservative position represents an important attack on the automatic response of bureaucracies to paper over crises. It is a position worth considering because it is true that, without government intervention, there simply would not be a protracted debt crisis. Loans would be rewritten, and life would go on. But those who oppose that position say that if we believe that government should intervene, because we are concerned with the side effects of a rewriting of the debts on the stability of the banking system, clearly the government, when intervening, should impose a settlement that takes into account broad social interests. But that has not, in fact, been the case. The crisis has been managed as if American interests were exclusively banking interests, a position conservatives rightly consider scandalous.

The writing down of bonds in the 1940s, in the aftermath of moratoria during the Great Depression, represents a good example of a market solution. In late 1943, Brazil implemented a unilateral exchange offer to consolidate debt service in a manner that is highly suggestive of possibilities today. The 1943 plan consolidated the entire Brazilian debt, stretched the maturities by forty to sixty years, and adjusted down both principal and interest. Creditors were offered a choice between two plans:

- Plan A: No reduction of principal, but interest rates were reduced from more than 6.5 percent to 3.375 (and less) with a provision for a sinking fund. Debt service (interest plus sinking fund) amounted to between 2.9 and 5.1 percent.
- Plan B: For every $1,000 of original bonds, bondholders would receive a cash payment of between $75 and $175 and a new bond with a face value of $800 (and $500 in some cases) and a coupon reduced to 3.75 percent. The bonds had no fixed maturity but were entitled to a sinking fund. Interest plus sinking fund amounted to a combined debt-service rate of 6.4 percent.

By early 1946, only 22 percent of bondholders had not assented to the exchange offer. Plan A had been chosen by 22 percent of the bondholders, and 56 percent had opted for Plan B. Interestingly, after the 1943 downward adjustment in terms, with repudiation threats removed, the bonds actually *increased* in value. From rock bottom in 1940, prices increased over the next ten years more than sevenfold, yielding a compound rate of return (interest plus capital gains) of 125 percent per year.

Hence the notion that Brazilian loans are unusually attractive. Of course, that leaves out the widows and orphans who sold out at the bottom.

The Activist Position

There are few plausible excuses for total, unqualified repudiation of a debt. One is the case of debts incurred before a revolutionary government takes over. The argument is that a government should not have to service a debt incurred by the old government largely in an effort to suppress a revolution. But international law does not clearly support this position, and pragmatists in the world capital market normally try to enforce these debts on the grounds that governments come and go and that debts are country debts, not government debts.

The more serious issue regards debt situations where a major diversion of public funds into private hands has taken place, with the active collaboration of the lenders. The Philippines under Marcos is a case in point. There can be little objection to the position that debts should be selectively reviewed and possibly paid out of diverted assets. That may be difficult in practice, but it is certainly worth trying. It is interesting to note that, in a policy of "review and selective repudiation," the Philippine government has already been able to identify some fraudulent loans and secure new agreements with the creditors in some instances.

Chile provides another case of debts arising from political problems. In an effort to secure the external financing necessary to maintain its control of the country, the Pinochet government has assumed an increasing amount of private debts to foreign banks instead of allowing default. Banks have encouraged this nationalization. It is doubtful that a successor government would be obliged to repay these political debts.

The most complex repudiation issue is insolvency because insolvency cannot be determined with certainty. How is it possible to know that a country will not, one day twenty or thirty years from now, for example, experience a marked turn toward the better and finally be in a position where debts can be serviced? Moreover, if debt service is only 10 or 20 percent of GDP then it *can* in principle be serviced. The only question is how to extract the debt service. In the area of sovereign debt the willingness and ability of a government to extract debt service from its citizens are important parts of the quality of debt, so insolvency often is primarily a political question.

John Maynard Keynes has persuasively argued that there is an important role for government initiative when contracts become uncollectible because uncollectible contracts place *extreme and unexpected* burdens on debtors. Society then should be willing to compromise the integrity of contracts, contrary to the usual rule.[7] Keynes argues against the absolute and unconditional validity of contracts:

> For nothing can preserve the integrity of a contract between individuals, except a discretionary authority in the State to revise what has become intolerable. The powers of uninterrupted usury are too great. If the accretion of vested interest were to grow without mitigation for many generations, half the population would be no better than slaves to the other half. . . . Those who insist that in these matters the State is in exactly the same position as an individual will, if they have their way, render impossible the continuance of an individualist society, which depends for its existence on moderation. . . . Changes in death duties, income tax, land tenure, licensing, game laws, church establishment, feudal rights, slavery, and so on through all ages, have received the same denunciations from the absolutist of contract, who are the real parents of revolution.[8]

Keynes's argument focuses on overly burdensome taxes used to service domestic debt, but the same argument applies to external debts. In the case of domestic debt, invalidating a contract affects income distribution within a country. But when international debts are at stake, the redistribution is between countries, and beyond the discretion of a single government. In the absence of world governments who could exercise the moderating function Keynes describes, debtor countries, in extreme situations, must decide whether or not to repudiate. Of course, they only will do so if they believe that whatever sanctions might be applied will cost less than the burden of continued debt service. Even so, repudiation can be justified only in extraordinary situations—Bolivia, Peru, and some countries in Africa.[9] Those circumstances are not the ones facing Brazil, Mexico, or even Argentina.

It is also important to emphasize that repudiation can be considered only if creditors stubbornly refuse to cooperate, which is, of course, a sensitive, delicate issue. The world's resources concentrate on the large debtors whose conduct has the greatest effect on bank stock market valuation and who attract the most political attention. Brazil or Mexico can command the attention and creativity of the IMF anytime and at the shortest notice. The same is not true for Ecuador or other small countries. Thus very few intellectual resources are devoted to those cases where responsible government intervention would be most helpful. It would not be surprising if, after being unnoticed for so long, some of these countries ultimately elect to default.

Chapter 7
Debt Politics

Debt problems make the headlines because they have all the ingredients of a good story. There is the populist story: poor, newly democratic countries undergo extraordinary social, economic, and political strains because powerful banks (with the help of the IMF and a conservative U.S. administration) are trying to extract debt service on a scale and at a rate that these countries simply cannot afford. According to this story, there is an urgent need for intervention to make broader national interests, including foreign policy interests, take precedence over debt collection. Those who advocate this view argue for debt forgiveness. The other story emphasizes the cliche of persistent and endless mismanagement of debtor countries. If only economic policies could be straightened out, the foreign assets of the residents of those countries could be mobilized to pay off much of the debt and restore growth. It is only the relentless inability of those nations to adjust that prevents a solution to the debt problem. Therefore, it would be blatant error to bail out—and even reward—policymakers in the debtor countries by offering debt relief or even new money.[1]

And, of course, there are also more moderate positions. One is that the debt problem needs enhanced political and regulatory supervision and intervention because financial institutions are vulnerable, overexposed, and have inadequate reserves with which to face an outright disruption of debt service.

Numerous groups with special interests have also taken positions in the debate. Trade interests are affected—and are becoming increasingly vocal. Debt service requires foreign exchange, which debtor countries earn by cutting down on their imports and by increasing exports. The United States, still hurt by the effect of an overvalued dollar, thus experiences additional trade problems as a result of the debt crisis.

The investment banking community has now entered the debate. Having seized on the opportunity to make a market in LDC loans by bringing together investors and banks who wish to sell out, the banking community is now eager to expand this new business, but expansion is possible only if the debtor countries open up to foreign capital on a massive scale. Hence the lobbying by the banking community for debt-equity swaps and a generally more favorable investment climate. There is also an interest in securitizing the debt—taking it out of the banks and selling it to the investing public.

And there are others in the debate: for example, the multilateral institutions, particularly the World Bank, which sees a unique opportunity to press for specific policy reforms and thus insists on conditionality when making loans.

The position of the debtor countries is that the restructuring process must be greatly simplified and speeded up. Above all they want recognition of the fact that development finance has been set back because now resources are flowing from developing regions to capital-rich countries.

The Reagan administration has chosen to get involved in the debt problem because of the implications for the banking system. Once the administration participated in the initial rescue efforts for Mexico, hardly a rescheduling has taken place that did not start with a visit by authorities of the debtor countries to the Treasury and the Federal Reserve, who define the broad outlines for the settlement. In some instances, such as Mexico's restructuring, the role of the administration is dominant. In others, such as Bolivia's, where no significant policy interests are at stake, the IMF is given the responsibility.

The administration has taken the position that debt management policies should follow a basically free market direction and that debt forgiveness must be ruled out. Thus changes in debt strategy, except for the rhetoric of the Baker Plan, have been repeatedly rejected. Assistant Secretary of the Treasury David Mulford told the House Banking Committee in March 1987:

> I recognize that a number of proposals have surfaced in recent months which assume that the debt strategy has failed. They all propose dramatic, large-scale solutions to the debt problem through short-term debt relief, with the objective of boosting both debtor nations' imports and U.S. exports.

These proposals range from outright debt and debt service forgiveness by both commercial banks and governments, to the creation of a new World Bank debt facility to purchase commercial bank debt at a deep discount from nominal value and then pass those savings on to debtor nations, to regulatory measures designed to force banks to write-off debt on their own books.

While such approaches may have some political appeal, they are impractical and ultimately counterproductive. Let me explain why such "grand gestures" are not feasible. . . .

Across the board debt forgiveness may have some limited appeal, but would ultimately damage both debtor nations and the global economy. External capital for debtors would not be available except perhaps at prohibitive prices; government dictated bank losses weaken our most important financial institutions; and U.S. budget and taxpayer costs would increase significantly.[2]

Former Secretary of the Treasury Baker explained the administration's position on any kind of forgiveness in the same terms:

I recognize that it is politically tempting to search for dramatic gestures which could sharply reduce debt service burdens overnight, or significantly increase the financial resources available to debtor nations to import our goods. Across-the-board debt forgiveness, in this light, may have some mistaken appeal, but would ultimately damage both debtor nations and the global economy. External capital would be available to debtors at prohibitive prices, if at all; bank losses would weaken some of our important financial institutions and U.S. budget and taxpayer costs would increase significantly.[3]

Another year of muddling through has changed nothing on this position. The Reagan administration position was reinforced by two considerations. First, the administration was nearing its end and thus could believe it politically advisable to leave these dramatic and confrontational issues for the next administration. Second, the U.S. budget problem makes any intervention by the U.S. taxpayer quite difficult. But without taxpayer participation, ambitious reforms are far less likely, certainly in the case of the major debtors.

There may be one exception to the refusal to consider forgiveness. An attempt at the 1987 Venice summit suggested the possibility of some debt forgiveness for the poorest African countries. At the 1988 summit in Toronto, on European insistence, partial debt relief for the poorest African countries was finally agreed upon. But it is worth noting that the relief fell short by far from being an effective measure; the debt relief merely slowed down the piling up of unpaid debts to official creditors.

Interestingly, it is not only the administration that is involved in debate on the debt crisis. Many members of Congress have also taken an interest in it. Other than the proximity of Mexico and a general foreign policy interest, it is not clear, at first, why a senator or congressman should be particularly interested or even go as far as to define a highly visible position. It is clear why a committee chairman for Southeast Asia would hold sympathetic hearings on the plight of the Philippines. But it is more difficult to pinpoint the motives of the senators and congressmen who have explored or actually proposed legislation for some form of debt relief or change in the debt management negotiations. The first and most visible, and given his political aspirations, most understandable, has been Senator Bill Bradley, who has been campaigning for a trade-debt package. But Senator Paul Sarbanes and Congressmen David Obey, Joe Kennedy, Charles Schumer, John LaFalce, Bruce Morrison, and Walter Fauntroy have also been sponsoring and participating in hearings and proposing legislation. Congressional interest has now gone beyond hearings.

The political efforts of this group have found expression in provisions of the trade bill requiring the administration to study the feasibility and advisability of an "International Debt Management Authority." The bill requires the secretary of the treasury to report his findings every six months and, unless a determination is made that a facility would be counterproductive, to initiate discussions with developing and industrialized countries to establish a debt management authority. It is worth noting that the bill provides quite explicitly "that such an authority should be designed to operate as a self-supporting entity, requiring no routine appropriation of resources from any member government."

While the inclusion of a debt management authority in the trade bill demonstrates that debt *is* a political issue, it must also be recognized that it is not a big one.

Most members of Congress do not get excited about debt and maintain their distance. The World Bank's general capital increase (GCI) got stuck in Congress on the issue whether World Bank loans could be used to help debtor countries pay interest to commercial bank creditors. The moderate Democrats won out in separating support for the World Bank from the debt issue, and the GCI went through basically without strings attached. In the 1988 presidential campaign, the debt issue did come up in the debates. Then Vice President Bush, when asked about the debt issue, reaffirmed that the Baker Plan was working fine, and Governor Dukakis used the question to discuss farm debt. But even if debt issues continue to be disregarded by most politicians, it is worth recording Senator Bradley's stern warning:

> The next President can't champion democracy in the world if his debt policies in Latin America impose austerity on farmers and workers who have never seen foreign currency, much less borrowed any. If he demands that those farmers and workers pay—in joblessness and hunger—for the mistakes of past regimes, he would betray the promise of democratic capitalism. The next President must master the conflict between debt and democracy or Latin America will master his foreign policy agenda.[4]

This congressional interest must be understood not only in terms of party politics but also in terms of traditional congressional politics on banking issues. Small and regional banks believe that they have been badly hurt by large money-center banks: defending their interests is good politics. There are several possible political reasons for proposing a balanced foreign policy position when the administration is seen as pushing to collect bank debts or ignoring an acute failure of its debt strategy. One is that linking trade and debt makes a good liberal position: it has anti-big-bank overtones and is suitably anti-administration while being responsible in terms of both foreign policy and the advocacy of sound financial institutions.

In some cases, rhetoric aside, the proposals were not far from the administration's position. Thus the Schumer Option Plan, which would allow banks to participate in a rescheduling without outright new money commitments, was no different from the "menu approach" advocated recently by the Treasury in the face of increasing fatigue of the creditors' cartel.[5]

Moreover, congressional commitment does not seem very strong: key committees have not moved legislation for major changes in the regulatory treatment of debt, and it does not look as if such moves are coming. This hesitancy is something Latin American leaders have long understood, and it is why they have not attempted to exploit the congressional interest in the debt problem.

We already saw that, on the international level, the Baker Plan remains the official answer, solemnly reaffirmed at the summit in Toronto. But that reaffirmation barely overshadowed increasing pressure by Japan to see some initiative. In an effort not to embarrass the U.S. administration in the run up to the election, the Japanese government has abstained so far from making any concrete proposal, but they have left little doubt about their wish to see action. As a current account surplus country under attack, Japan is looking for opportunities to score points. Nothing is safer than proposing an impressive-sounding capital recycling program. As long as the United States, West Germany, and Britain oppose the idea, there are no costs and only benefits from seeming less intransigent. If the other countries do decide to go ahead, Japan could not stay out, but at least will have the benefit of claiming it promoted the deal. In any event, at this stage no concrete proposals have emerged nor have any been appropriated by the Japanese parliament.

The political interests behind the various proposals for easing the debt crisis are so varied that no major change in the debt strategy is likely unless debtor countries themselves bring it about. But it is worth examining the alternative schemes of debt consolidation that have been suggested to see if they hold any promise before making an argument for unilateral action on the part of the debtors.

Chapter 8
Debt Consolidation

Most of the proposals for handling the debt crisis spell out in intricate detail how payments should be reduced or tied to this or that. Few proposals, however, explicitly recognize that who pays—the debtor, the bank stockholder, Japan, or the taxpayer—is the central issue. The current deadlock is a result of the failure to reach an agreement about who will bear the costs of ending the debt crisis, and almost equally important, who must take the initiative to change the current system.

It is easy for the debtor countries to advocate debt relief. Their position is unambiguous: the harsh world macroeconomic environment, especially the continuing high interest rates, is responsible for the continuation of the debt crisis. Debt relief is appropriate, and the industrial countries should provide it. Moreover, debt relief should be unconditional. They do not care whether it comes out of the pocket of bank stockholders or taxpayers. For them, debt is a political issue.

On the creditor side, the discussion is not much more enlightened. The idea that the U.S. taxpayer should bail out banks that have made loans to governments that proceeded to use those loans to finance capital flight and overspending is rejected outright. Why should we bail out Mexicans if we don't bail out our own farmers?

No wonder the discussion of relief never gets off the ground. Dealing with the debt problem in those terms obscures the fact that cutting real wages in half in order to secure debt service can be political dynamite and that limited, targeted, selective debt relief may be in everybody's interest.

The critical question is how to provide debt relief. There are basically two directions worth exploring: a change in the regulatory environment (to ease the costs to banks of limited, selective write-offs or concessions), or the creation of an international facility to buy up and/or guarantee developing-country debts, securing limited debt relief in the process.

Changing the Regulatory Environment

Granting Spontaneous Relief. The very unfavorable, or at least ambiguous, regulatory environment is one reason banks hesitate to discuss debt relief. At present, granting debt relief to a particular country would endanger the entire principal and require reserve provisions and accounting losses. This situation reveals the absurdity of a regulatory system under which making loans better (in the sense of reducing the probability of repudiation) forces a write-down, while hard-line collection does not, even if it reduces the secondary-market valuation.

These regulations may be a result of a strategy of raising the costs of concessions to banks. But they also tempt the banks to play chicken, which may ultimately prove more expensive than a more open system, where banks and debtor countries can negotiate write-offs in return for promises to improve their economic policies.

The same regulatory issue arises in respect to the sale of claims at less than face value. If a bank should sell off part of its claims on a particular country in the secondary market, the regulatory authorities now require that the remaining part of the debt be written down by the discount at which the debt was sold. That makes the banks increasingly reluctant to sell, limiting the growth of the market.[1] It implies that developing-country debt remains trapped in the wrong places, making the rescheduling process much more tedious.

Another source of ambiguity is the role of taxpayers. If there were a chance that the taxpayer could come to the rescue, directly or via a sharply increased funding of the World Bank or a new institution, it would be clearly premature for either side to talk of concessions. Countries should borrow rather than adjust, and banks should lend at as high interest rates as possible. Establishing a precommitment that defines the limits on the role of the taxpayer, while difficult, is necessary if voluntary deals between banks and debtors are to be encouraged.

Three points need to be clarified in connection with the role of banks in rescheduling. One is to denounce the myth that banks in the aggregate have the option of not lending to the debtors. That is possible only if the debtors can and are willing to earn enough through trade surpluses to pay all the interest on their debts. Failing that, in order to be paid the interest due them, banks have to lend the debtors enough to allow them to meet those payments. Not lending means not receiving the interest payments—and ultimately writing off the loans.

The second point is the implication for debtors of increased loan-loss reserves. A bank that sets aside loan-loss reserves or even writes down loans does not, by so doing, grant debt relief. These are measures taken for regulatory or prudential reasons, or as a strategic move in interbank competition. But write-downs do not by themselves benefit debtor countries. Even after write-downs, banks still intend to collect the loans. They merely recognize, for regulatory purposes, that the loans are behind schedule or are doubtful.

The third point concerns the role of loan-loss reserves in the bargaining between banks and debtors. The view that banks become stronger as a result of increased reserves is balanced by the fact that debtors will no longer feel that they might bring down the world financial system if they were to take a more aggressive negotiating position. It is not clear which of these points is most important, and all three deserve recognition in the context of increases in loan-loss reserves in the aftermath of the dramatic move by Citicorp in 1987.

Interest Capitalization. Some Swiss bankers have recommended the *automatic* capitalization of interest payments at the discretion, for the most part, of the debtor.[2] The system is designed to minimize the possibility of confrontation between the banks and a debtor when a country suffers a liquidity crisis, thus eliminating any plausible excuse for default. The proposal runs directly counter to the concerns of U.S. banks that insist on the full current payment of interest and reject capitalization.

In the Swiss proposal, the counterpart of automatic capitalization is a set of objective indicators that trigger enhanced debt service. For example, if oil prices exceed a particular level, an oil-exporting nation would be required to use its increased revenues to bring payments of interest up to date—and perhaps even to start amortizing principal.

This plan is attractive to the European banks, which, since they have set aside reserves amounting to a large part of their claims, consider any receipts good news. The U.S. banks, which, in contrast, are very concerned with quarterly receipts, end up severely aggravating the debt problem by forcing debtor countries into much more dramatic adjustments. The Swiss plan improves the quality of debts by relaxing the timing of interest rate receipts, and it eliminates the risk of default by a debtor facing excessive insistence on current service. But at the same time, the scheme also means that creditors forgo some of the control that they now exert through the adjustment programs required for rescheduling. There might be a middle ground between the concern of U.S. bankers about quarterly interest payments and the infinite horizon of a Swiss banker.

The automatic interest capitalization proposal is very different from a proposal of a cap on interest payments, say, at 6 percent, with the excess automatically forgiven. Under the former scheme, the portion of the debt that is capitalized retains an option value should matters improve; in other words, banks give concessions today in order to get a payback down the road.

At present, when debtor countries cannot service their debts, creditor banks grant them loans as new money to use to pay the interest. Under the concessions provisions of an automatic capitalization, the difficulty and confrontation involved in rescheduling and the problem of organizing the new loans disappear. The plan locks all creditors into refinancing in a way that is now impossible. And, perhaps most important, the plan allows the debtors to do more long-term planning by eliminating the threat that, if a country cannot work out a rescheduling agreement with its creditors, it will have to choose between a dramatic depression or an equally dramatic default. Living with that kind of uncertainty has proved harmful to investment and to growth.

The International Facility

In 1983, Peter Kenen presented a proposal for a special facility to take over developing-country debts from the banks so that the stock of old, bad debt would no longer stand in the way of a resumption of lending.[3] The facility would operate with donated capital or government guarantees, which, of course, overtly involve the taxpayers in the industrialized countries in debt relief. The new public body created would be charged with the task of bringing about renewed resource flows to debtor countries. An obvious way to do this would be to buy up debt of problem debtors in the secondary market, and then turn the claim over to the debtor country in exchange for a bond with a long-term maturity and a pattern of interest disbursements that would help support the debtor country's adjustment program.

A similar proposal by Richard Weinert calls for a sponsoring agency, the World Bank or the U.S. government, to issue its own debt and exchange it with a bank for a claim on a developing country on a dollar-for-dollar basis.[4] The sponsor's bond would carry a lower interest rate, low enough that its market value, as opposed to face value, would reflect the difference between this interest rate and the market for U.S. Treasury bills. The size of the interest rate reduction would be such that the present value of the bond would carry a discount equal to the market discount. Banks that agree to the swap take a loss on the interest rate but acquire in place of a developing-country bond of questionable worth a risk-free government bond. The sponsor in turn converts the debt acquired from the banks into a claim on the developing country that exactly matches the bond issued to the bank.

It is important to remember that the discount in the secondary market reflects not only the inability of debtors to pay but also their unwillingness to do so. Therefore, Weinert's scheme would require that the participating countries accept adjustment programs aimed at improving their international payments position. Under this arrangement, those countries whose debts trade at the largest discounts—Bolivia or Peru, for example—would get the most debt relief. The sponsors—really the taxpayers of the countries supporting the scheme—assume the default risk, the debtor gets the full benefit of the implicit bank write-off in the form of interest relief, and the bank restores its balance sheet by acquiring low-yield, safe claims in place of precarious ones.

There is no free lunch in this scheme. The taxpayer assumes the default risk or else there is no way of reaping the benefits of the discount. To be sure, debt relief in the form of lower interest rates or reduced principal reduces the burdens of debtors. But the debt reduction from a few billion of these swaps may not be enough to reduce the risk of default or the risk of payments difficulties to near-zero. Henry Kaufman, a well-known Wall Street economist, makes the same point about a similar plan he has proposed. Kaufman's plan also involves converting debt into marketable securities at a discount indicated by the secondary-market price:

> Despite the debt relief provided by this plan, the debtor countries would not be restored to creditworthiness initially. As a result, the securitized debt would still tend to trade at a substantial discount to face value in the early years. Therefore, in order to induce investors to hold these securities, some form of guarantee would be helpful. Such a guarantee need not fully cover the face value of the new security, but rather, might only cover longer-dated payments.[5]

The most detailed plan so far has been advanced by the chairman of American Express, James Robinson III.[6] His proposal envisages a mandatory sale of developing-country debt by banks to an International Debt and Development Institute in exchange for guaranteed paper and with a possible participation in the ultimate proceeds from loan liquidation. The institute in turn would renegotiate the debts, choosing a debt-service profile that made sense in the context of an agreed adjustment program, including trade liberalization. There would be debt reduction in exchange for adjustment performance.

An American Fund. A possible solution to the debt problem might be a fund that buys the debt of all countries, other than the four major debtors, from U.S. banks. There would be a quota—determined by economic and political considerations—for each debtor country. The purpose of excluding the four major debtors is to assure that scarce budget resources be used with maximum effect. On that count, a dollar of debt relief for Bolivia is worth far more than a dollar of relief for Brazil. The line is drawn to include the Philippines in the program, thus assuring increased chances of political success.

The fund would try to restructure the commercial bank debt of very poor and small debtors, even if that meant buying up the debts held by foreign banks. This plan would allow small U.S. banks to get out of their debts to these nations by easing banking regulations.

The debt to U.S. banks, excluding Venezuela, Argentina, Brazil, and Mexico but including the Philippines, amounts to $16 billion, and the average secondary-market discount is in excess of 50 percent. Suppose a fund were organized that in fact captures the full discount and passes it on as debt reduction. The $8 billion decline in debt to U.S. banks would represent a sizable reduction of total debt, perhaps as much as 20 percent. And this could be done with a guarantee that hardly needs to exceed $2 billion and may never be called. If the rules for participation in the fund are well structured (giving the fund a share in any favorable developments in debtor countries and giving them a break in unfavorable situations), a relatively small guarantee commitment can, in fact, buy an astounding reversal in the domestic and external stability and prospect for a host of small countries while relieving banks of increasingly uncollectable and deteriorating debt.

U.S. policymakers are extremely concerned about the destabilizing influence Nicaragua is playing in Central America, but they are not sufficiently aware that the debt collection process is also causing a deterioration in economic and political stability in other Central American countries, eventually weakening their stability. This is the case in Ecuador as much as it is in Costa Rica.

The U.S. budget would have to absorb the contingent liability involved in underwriting the bonds issued by the fund but serviced by the income from developing-country debts. If there were defaults, the U.S. government would have to assume debt service. At one time the federal government gave such guarantees quite freely, but now it is harder to get approval and appropriations from Congress. Thus, if the facility were to be operated by the U.S. government, it would have to survive congressional budget review.

There are, of course, other possible sources of support for such a facility. One is the World Bank. The industrial countries with strong currencies and external surpluses are another. In fact, many observers have looked to Japan as a candidate for assuming the guarantees necessary. Support from such countries is the gist of the proposal by James Robinson III of American Express and of the recommendation of Senator Sarbanes and a number of other congressmen.

A Special Role for the Facility. If a new facility were set up, it could also play a role in debt negotiations. The fund would get involved in rescheduling agreements to assure that the value of its assets was not impaired by extortionary settlements or unreasonable adjustment programs. The facility might even make available a long-term reconstruction loan to a particular country. In exchange for participating in the financing, it would secure from the banks extraordinary reductions in spreads or maturities. If the facility is to take this aggressive a role, the head of the organization will have to be independent, beyond the immediate reach of the U.S. Treasury.

The bottom line though remains the participation of the taxpayer, who must provide the capital or at least the guarantees. The role of the taxpayer in the industrial countries may be hidden by having the World Bank do the borrowing, or it may be as close to the front page as pressure on Japan to do something about the debt problem. But unless the taxpayer takes over the default risk in some way, debtors will not get the full advantage of the discounts at which the debts are now traded.

It is fashionable to argue that the taxpayer cannot get involved. But that, of course, overlooks the fact that the taxpayer is already fully engaged. Tax losses from reduced U.S. exports and reduced earnings of U.S. corporations have already occurred, and a severe deterioration in

Latin American political security would amount to a major burden on the U.S. budget. For the taxpayer, therefore, choice must be how best to commit resources. An American fund may well dominate the Baker Plan.

The Menu or Options Approach

A number of other proposals for solving the debt crisis have been put forth in the past several months. Most are various combinations of the three proposals that have already been examined. Congressman Charles Schumer and the Treasury have argued for providing a range of options that would make rescheduling more flexible. Rather than requiring commercial banks to participate in restructuring on the basis of their August 1982 share in lending exposure to a particular country, this new approach suggests the possibility of exit bonds, debt-equity swaps, and any other arrangements.

But these have been tried before: the Argentine rescheduling provided incentives for early signing on, special exit bonds, debt-equity swaps, and an investment fund.[7] The options approach is an important development because it makes rescheduling more flexible, but it does not solve the basic problem of net resource transfers.

Debt Buy-backs. In the aftermath of the Mexican buy-back attempt the idea that this mechanism could provide a major route for debt reduction is thriving. A buy-back involves some combination of cash payments and substitution of new bonds with credit enhancement for the old debt. The discussion of this mechanism has clearly led to two conclusions. First, a successful buy-back operation either requires cash that problem debtors (by definition) do not have, or it requires *seniority* for the new instrument that is traded in at a discount for the existing debt. Second, if cash is used, it is essential to ask whether debt reduction is the best use an illiquid country can make of its scarce foreign exchange resources.[8]

The most recent example of using market-related, voluntary means of debt reduction was the Morgan-Mexico attempt at debt conversion. Creditors were offered at auction, in exchange for their claims, a new bond with a guaranteed principal (via a zero-coupon, twenty-year U.S. government bond) but with interest payments that did not command seniority over the existing debt. The discounts at which the debt conversion took place were not significantly different from the secondary-market valuation, except for the recognition of the guaranteed principal. The debt reduction that was achieved was disappointingly modest.

When a debt conversion is based, as was the case for Mexico, on substituting new debt for old debt, seniority has to go much further than implicit understandings about prior claims on a debtor's resources. To achieve significant discounts in debt exchange, the seniority has to be recognized and supported, if not enforced, by industrial-country governments or their agencies. Proposals for World Bank action in supplying credit enhancement in the form of rolling one-year interest guarantees have recently emerged as the prototype of such seniority.

The Mexican exchange offer, and the earlier Bolivian buy-back operation that took place with the support of creditor countries and the IMF, has also raised the question of whether this is the best use a country can make of available resources. These resources have an alternative use in liberalizing imports or supporting investment and growth. Debt reduction can be the less interesting investment. But that need not be the case if a debt overhang massively deteriorates macroeconomic stability and the profitability of investment. But in hindsight that was not the case for Mexico or Brazil. In Mexico, reserves were used for buybacks that only a few months later were badly needed to keep the stabilization program afloat. A U.S. emergency bridge loan had to restore the resources that were dissipated in the debt exchange earlier in the year. In Brazil's case, debt reduction was financed by printing money. In this case the alternative was not to have a hyperinflation, clearly a preferable strategy to what has in fact occurred.

In summary, there are no effective and comprehensive market-related mechanisms of debt reduction. Taxpayers are unwilling to underwrite debtor country growth. The Reagan administration was reluctant to change its debt strategy, which was based on free market principles of adjustment and a policy of no debt forgiveness. The banks are putting money into reserves against their debtor-country loans, but they will not consider write-offs so long as there is no outright default, and even then are likely to wait to see whether the government will pick up the tab. In the meantime, the debt problem continues; there are frequent reschedulings and uncertainties, and economic and social conditions in the debtor countries are deteriorating as net resource transfers go from poor countries to rich countries rather than the other way around.

Chapter 9
Conclusion: A Proposal for Mexican Debt

Policymakers in developed countries insist that the Baker Plan is the best available option. They claim no better idea has come up, and they make the point that debtor countries themselves chose to cooperate in the process. Brazil is used as the most striking example. After a year in a state of moratorium, Brazil returned to negotiations with the banks and signed on to a rescheduling agreement the generosity of which more than made up for the stigma of the previous moratorium. Secretary Baker approvingly quotes Paul Volcker's support for the Baker Plan and Brazil's march of penance:

> I note with interest that just last week, Paul Volcker, in comments on the debt strategy, reportedly observed that "there's been a tendency among academics and the media to pronounce the plan dead. They've had six years to think of another approach," he added, "and they haven't been able to come up with one." The strategy remains, he concluded, the only effective method in sight.
>
> Brazil's announcement this month struck the same chord. It stated that "the time has come to normalize our relations with the international financial community" because the absence of good relations was bad for Brazil. This resolute act acknowledged the costs of the past policy, the need for economic adjustment, and the importance of gaining international financial support for growth and development. While this is but a step in a progressive restoration of mutually valuable ties, it is a good and sensible stride forward.[1]

The recent $3.5 billion bridge loan to Mexico is yet another demonstration that the system does work in the sense of keeping debts afloat and persuading major debtors to stay in the process. The constant threat of unilateral moves is carefully checked and abated by emergency measures just sufficient to justify debtor countries' decisions to stay on the treadmill. But staying in the process has become an end in itself; it does nothing to help a country to achieve growth nor does it strengthen social and political progress.

What is essential is a plan for a unilateral action with two characteristics: First, it puts a priority on a sustained, market-oriented growth in debtor countries. Second, in the long run it represents a more plausible assurance that creditors will be paid the full value of their claims. In putting growth and financial stability first, this approach represents a radical departure from the Baker Plan, which tried to keep loans current even at the cost of extreme instability in debtor countries. Mexico is the country best placed to take a responsible unilateral measure to change the debt process from a mechanism for outward transfers to one that brings about sharply increased investment in the domestic economy. A policy of interest recycling (essentially debt-equity swaps on the interest payments rather than the principal) can achieve this goal in some cases. A policy of interest recycling can alleviate the foreign exchange problems associated with debt service and in that way help remove financial uncertainty, which today is one of the major obstacles to a resumption of investment in debtor countries.

The Two Transfer Problems as a Guide. The debt crisis, as noted earlier, creates two difficulties for debtors, the budgetary problem and the foreign exchange or dollar problem. The budget problem arises when a debtor cannot raise enough taxes, or cut public spending sufficiently, to finance the interest payments on the debt. Deficit finance and high inflation, as occurred in Brazil or Argentina, are the typical results. The dollar problem emerges if a country cannot bring about (by recession or real depreciation) a sufficient trade surplus to earn the dollars required for debt service. This leads to uncertainty about the future exchange rates, which often translates into capital flight and hence even worse foreign exchange problems.

It is essential to recognize that among debtors there are significant differences in their *relative* exposure to these two problems. Table 9-1 shows four cases and brings out the fact that Argentina suffers from both problems, whereas Korea (another major debtor) has neither; Brazil has

Table 9-1
The Two Transfer Problems

		Dollar Problem	
		Yes	No
Budget Problem	Yes	Argentina	Brazil
	No	Mexico	Korea

a very strong external balance (because of recession, high commodity prices, and low oil prices) but suffers an extremely large budget deficit and near-hyperinflation. Mexico, by contrast, has solved the budget problem but, because of import liberalization and low oil prices, has a very precarious external balance position. Across-the-board debt reduction is not the appropriate response to so much diversity. It is clear from the variety of cases that a case-by-case approach will better solve the specific problem of a debtor country.

Over the past three years, Mexico has brought the budget under control. Even with oil prices low, the government's accounts are almost balanced. This situation contrasts sharply with the large deficits in Brazil and Argentina. The contrast highlights the fact that even when a country has brought its fiscal affairs under control, as Mexico has, the debt crisis continues to be a major threat to financial stability because of the external transfer problem. The risks of yet further depreciation of the exchange rate, and the resulting domestic political and economic instability as labor seeks to avoid real wage cuts, are a constant invitation for capital flight. The slightest news of a deterioration of the trade balance translates into waves of capital flight. Until the dollar problem is solved, or effectively suspended, the economy maintains a short horizon and is unwilling to invest in anything except paper assets. As a result, growth cannot take place even if fundamentals are right. There is a coordination problem in shifting the economy to an investment mood, and debt service can be made a key lever in effecting the change.

The Proposal: A plan for solving the Mexican growth problem involves three components:

- For a ten-year period, part of the debt service, say 55 percent, is paid in pesos. These pesos can be used for unrestricted investment in Mexico. The only restriction is that creditors cannot repatriate them. In exchange, the Mexican government undertakes to liberalize and facilitate investment legislation to remove any remaining obstacles. After ten years, the principal and accumulated earnings can be withdrawn according to a phased program at the official exchange rate.

• A portion of the debt service is automatically capitalized, say 25 percent, and in this way helps finance a moderate recovery of public sector investment. The rate of interest paid on these loans is equal to the U.S. rate of inflation plus the rate of growth of Mexican per capita income. The return guarantees that foreign creditors participate in any upswing of the Mexican economy, while avoiding at the same time a ballooning of debt-service obligations relative to long-run ability to pay.

• A portion equal to 20 percent of debt service continues to be made in dollars, thus assuring creditors of some dollar earnings.

The Mexican authorities would, in addition, facilitate the securitization of claims so that it becomes possible to divide the debt among the three options to suit individual creditors' preferences for investment opportunities, capitalization, or current cash.

What Does the Plan Achieve? The plan assures that the risk of exchange depreciation is eliminated or at least made far more remote. With a sharp reduction in the amount of *dollars* required for debt service, it now beomes possible to have growth *and* financial stability. The major portion of interest payments is now invested by commercial banks in the Mexican economy. This directly increases investment in plant and equipment because credit restrictions ease and loans for firms become available on more acceptable terms. Investors who were waiting for a concrete signal of change, from stagnation to growth, will see the coordinated investment thrust in the financial system as exactly that signal.

But the turnaround in expectations is not limited to the home economy. The private sector, which now holds extensive assets abroad, will soon recognize that capacity expansion and increases in asset prices signal a turnaround for the economy. They will repatriate their assets (cautiously, gradually, but nevertheless they will do so) in order not to miss out on the expansion. Interest recycling thus is equivalent to jump-starting a car: if the fundamentals are right it works, and soon the economy can move on its own. But without the jump-start, no amount of persuasion or gas will get it moving.

It is instructive to view Mexico's problems in the perspective of a bank run. As long as creditors insist on collecting their full claims *now,* the bank is illiquid and must suspend disbursements; private capital flight acts to magnify the illiquidity. But if bank creditors are willing to freeze their claims for a while, the bank can function and even attract an external reflow. The capitalization and recycling of interest payments are thus the coordinating device equivalent to a bank closing. It is done in the very interest of the creditors to avoid a deterioration of their claims. Put another way, if Mexico cannot recover growth and financial stability there is no chance that creditors will be paid, year after year, for the next decades. But with growth there is not even a presumption that Mexico is insolvent; on the contrary, we might well find that ten years from now a much stronger Mexico, integrated into the U.S. manufacturing market, has insignificant foreign exchange problems and attracts enough foreign exchange to allow an orderly liquidation of the debt overhang.

The scheme attacks directly the key bottleneck in the Mexican economy, foreign exchange. In 1987–88 there was a trade surplus that generated the dollars to transfer to foreign creditors. Under the recycling and capitalization scheme these transfers would be reduced by 80 percent; the foreign exchange thus freed would then be used to finance extra imports and to close the gap left by much lower oil prices. Unless foreign exchange can be found for this purpose there is a growing expectation of depreciation and a depletion of any remaining reserves by capital flight. That situation was entirely apparent in late 1988 when an urgent U.S. bridge loan was required merely to slow down the flight of capital.

Some Issues: Compared to What? There are several practical issues that need to be discussed. The first is the common objection that such a scheme is inflationary. Yes, it is inflationary by comparison with a policy of not paying *any* interest at all. But that is not the case with Mexico. Mexico is eager to, and has in fact in 1986–87, paid full interest. The budget has been improved sufficiently to finance the full interest payments out of taxes and spending cuts. In the budget, therefore, recycling is no different from what happens at present. There is clearly no extra inflationary impact.

The second concern is whether the Mexican government would accept so large an investment by foreign creditors in the Mexican economy. There is certainly an issue here, and any friendliness toward foreign investment is recent and tenuous. But it is also worthwhile asking what the alternatives are. Of course, not paying anything is a nationalist-populist response that involves none of *these* costs. But if the past is an indication, Mexico does want to stay largely within the system. In that case recycling and capitalization are far better ways of bringing about growth than further programs of real depreciation (under IMF auspices), which would increase the pauperization of the workers and middle class and aggravate political instability. A shift toward growth, and the actual experience of growth, quickly dissipates the most active criticism of foreign investment. But it is also worth noting that the capitalized portion of interest is in no way different from the current "new money" practice; the only difference is that it is automatic rather than being a confrontational, uncertain, and drawn-out procedure.

The third question is how banks could weather such a change in regime. Here, too, one must ask compared to what. Compared to a system of full, punctual debt service, the proposed regime represents a drastic deterioration. Banks, rather than debtor countries, now become illiquid. They would have to find ways of securitizing their claims and selling them off in the market (calling them the Mexico Fund). But that is not unreasonable because the banks do have free access to and the intellectual resources for operation in the world capital market. They are therefore much better equipped than debtor countries to suffer illiquidity pending the reconstruction effort. They are also the full beneficiaries of such a reconstruction. Of course, there is a need for regulatory changes to recognize the illiquidity of these loans. Cooperation of banks in the scheme should not be punished by adverse regulatory consequences. On the contrary, cooperation should be seen as improving the quality of otherwise very poor claims.

The fourth question is how to bring such a scheme about. Certainly banks have not advanced such a proposal, nor have international agencies or U.S. authorities. They all prefer the status quo simply because large moves are risky, while myopia allows them to believe that on the current course matters might improve. There is no alternative but responsible, unilateral action by Mexico. Once the proposal is on the table, with no active alternative, creditors are forced to make the best of it.

Finally there is the question whether such a proposal can also be used in other debtor countries. If a Mexican implementation is successful there is little doubt that it will provide an incentive for other countries that want to pay to make budget corrections and for market reforms that create a sustainable investment climate. Once that is done, and even as part of such a reform program, some mix of the three components can be developed that matches the specific country's needs.

Risks of the Strategy. This unilateral strategy is not risk-free. For example, once accepted by the creditors, the program may lead to a waste of resources. Large government spending and raises in real wages bring growth, but that just creates more debt problems. Mexico must use the breathing room provided by its unilateral debt consolidation to restore supply-side growth, which is long-term growth.

The threat used against unilateral action is sanctions. But realistically, there is very little that could be done to a country like Mexico if it chooses that path. The only concrete sanction would be a denial of trade credit, which could lead to a disruption of normal trade flows for a period of, perhaps, up to three months. The risk of trade credit drying up is more serious when inventories are low and foreign exchange reserves are depleted. But even here the costs are only temporary. In the case of Peru, following its unilateral decision to limit debt service to only 10 percent of exports, trade did not come to a standstill. On the contrary, countertrade and financing by multinational firms took over where banks were no longer lending.[2]

Another issue is whether a debtor country taking unilateral action faces the possibility of exclusion from world capital markets. If history is any guide, such an exclusion is not a danger. All of Latin America took unilateral action, ranging from moratoria to outright defaults, in the 1930s. Few paid more than 50 cents on the dollar, and all returned to voluntary borrowing. In fact, Latin American countries have defaulted many times in the past. Thus there is little reason to believe that there is no credit after unilateral action.

A more serious question is how long a return to voluntary lending will take. Three years or thirty years? It certainly depends on how much history investors remember and how attractive the lending opportunities look. No doubt, insurance companies and pension funds are in line to be the next lenders: the question in their case is when.

It is equally important to recognize that there is not going to be a quick return to voluntary lending. For commercial banks, exposure reduction in all of Latin America seems to be the rule, independent of past debt-service performance. As a result, it is unlikely that commercial banks or anyone else will return to lending in Latin America on a significant scale in the next few years. As commercial banks see it, the idea of voluntary lending is that Colombia should float bonds in the world capital market and use the proceeds to pay bank interest. Nobody expects these countries to be able to borrow enough money to pay interest *and* finance investment.

The return to voluntary lending appears remote, there are no effective sanctions for a major debtor, and creditor countries do not seem very interested in promoting change. And even if there were interest in change, a deadlock would result because neither Congress nor the administration can easily force the banks to grant a reduction in debt burdens, and the banks are unlikely to volunteer to do so. Under these circumstances, debtor countries need to look after their own interests.

Creditors' Interests. The suspension of resource transfers abroad does not mean that creditors are left stranded. The payments would be recycled into the debtor economies as new investments. Debtor countries have to make a commitment to free resources in their budget to actually pay the creditors. There can be no question of simply inflating away the interest payments. They also must overcome nationalism to create a climate that would permit them to turn the local currency payments into profitable, inflation-proof investments.

Growth and financial stability in Mexico, Brazil, or the Philippines would help create a business climate where investment can be profitable. With any luck, ten years later all the debt can be paid routinely out of the reflow of flight capital and spontaneous foreign investment. Even if it is not a sure thing, it is a more promising way to get one's money back than putting debtor countries into depression and hyperinflation.

Conclusion

The debt problem will not be solved until a major debtor thoughtfully and responsibly defines *unilaterally* the terms of debt consolidation.

In Brazil's case there is an obvious need for serious domestic stabilization and rebuilding of confidence in sustainable growth policies to accompany a change in debt service. Mexico's case for a change in the debt strategy is already more compelling. All the necessary adjustments in the budget have already occurred, and in that sense the country is prepared for a resumption of stable growth. But growth is incompatible with the large trade surpluses required to service the debt. To avoid a loss of confidence as growth gets under way and cuts into the trade surplus, it is essential to have a long-run debt strategy in place. Recycling offers the best prospect for debtor and creditor alike.

The rule so far has been that, unlike in the 1930s, no country should take unilateral steps. But it is clear now, after five years of muddling through, that the debt problems are worsening. It is also apparent that debt relief will have to be forced on creditors by debtors. Responsible unilateral action is therefore unavoidable—and, ultimately, welcome.

How should the governments of creditor countries react to such a unilateral measure? The administration's muddling-through strategy is stuck on a treadmill of pretense and make-believe in which both debtors and creditors are falling behind. When Mexican debt trades at 50 cents on the dollar, and that of Peru at less than a dime, the debt crisis is obviously unresolved. The debtors cannot afford to pay, nor can they afford to walk out on the system. Creditors are unwilling to provide new money. The result is a public interest in breaking the deadlock.

Debtor-country rhetoric has been that debt service has stopped growth and investment in their economies. Creditors keep telling us about the wonderful investment opportunities (for others) in developing countries. The recycling proposal takes up the challenge. Debtors get the resources to support reconstruction, but they cannot dissipate them by poor fiscal policies or premature growth of consumption. Creditors are put on hold, but their claims are enhanced by a sharply improved business climate and growth performance in the debtor countries. Surely our public interest, whether from the point of view of trade or foreign policy, is better served by debtor-country reconstruction than by the Baker treadmill.

As long as the action is limited and accompanied by strong positive steps to enhance the prospects for sustained growth and an ultimate ability to service the debt in dollars, it should be welcomed. Anything that gets the debtor countries, the banks, and the world economy out of the current impasse should be applauded.

In the summer of 1982, Silva Herzog, the Mexican finance minister, came to Washington to report that his country could not service its debts. In the midst of confusion and a flurry of rescue activity, he received one clear message: Above all, do not take unilateral action.[3] Now, six years later, we have come full circle: Someone, please do just that.

Notes

Chapter 1

1. The group of fifteen heavily indebted countries includes: Argentina, Bolivia, Brazil, Chile, Colombia, Ivory Coast, Ecuador, Mexico, Morocco, Nigeria, Peru, Philippines, Uruguay, Venezuela, and Yugoslavia. The World Bank list includes two further countries, Costa Rica and Jamaica.

2. See International Monetary Fund, *International Capital Markets*, January 1988, and *World Economic Outlook*, October 1988.

3. This point can be better understood by noting the relation between private saving and investment, the budget, and the noninterest balance:

Investment − Saving = Noninterest Deficit + Budget Surplus

The equation shows that resource transfers through a noninterest deficit can supplement the excess of investment over saving, but also that they may simply finance a public sector deficit. The latter may well be productively spent on infrastructure investment or investment in public sector enterprises. But it may also involve wasteful spending on monuments or defense.

4. External interest payments are financed either by a noninterest surplus or by a net capital inflow.

External Interest Payments = Noninterest Surplus + Net Capital Inflow

The net capital inflow may take one of four forms: a run-down of reserves, a repatriation of private capital, direct investment, or increased external borrowing from governments, multilateral institutions, or private creditors.

Chapter 2

1. See Morgan Guaranty, *World Financial Markets* (1986). In response to the dramatic inflation problem, the Federal Reserve changed its operating procedures to target money growth rather than interest rates and steered a sharply contractionary course. As a result of this policy change, interest rates increased to unprecedented levels.

Interest Rates and Inflation in World Trade

	1978	1979	1980	1981	1982	1983
LIBOR	8.9	12.1	14.2	16.9	13.3	9.7
Effective Rate [a]		9.1	11.8	13.4	13.5	10.7
Inflation [b]	12.7	15.5	20.3	− 3.8	− 3.5	− 3.3

Source: Author's calculations.

a. Interest payments as a fraction of debt outstanding for countries with recent debt-servicing problems.

b. Inflation of industrial countries' export prices.

The table brings out the shift in real interest rates from 1980 to 1981. It is difficult to judge the appropriate rate of inflation to use in measuring real interest rates. Clearly U.S. inflation is inappropriate, since the debtor countries are neither buying nor selling the U.S. consumer basket. Using the inflation rate of their export prices would lead to an excessively large increase of the real interest rate they faced. A balance is struck by using the export unit value of industrial countries as a measure of inflation. Since industrial country export prices have been declining in absolute terms since 1980, the real interest rates calculated with this index become positive. In fact, on this basis the real interest rate turns from - 5 percent in 1980 to +20 percent in 1981.

The increase in real interest rates is of approximately the same order of magnitude when one considers the effective rate rather than LIBOR. From - 10 percent it increases to +16 percent.

2. E. Wiesner, "Latin American Debt: Lessons and Pending Issues," *American Economic Review* 75, no. 2 (May 1985), p. 191.

3. Statement by Ciro DeFalco, U.S. Treasury, to a conference cosponsored by the Joint Economic Committee and the Congressional Research Service, *Dealing with the Debt Problem of Latin America,* 1986, p. 76.

4. B. Nowzad and R. Williams, *External Indebtedness of Developing Countries* (Washington, D.C.: International Monetary Fund, May 1, 1981), p. 1.

5. F. Mendelsohn, *The Outlook for International Bank Lending* (New York: Group of Thirty, 1981), pp. 20-21.

6. See C. Lewis, *America's Stake in International Investment* (Washington, D.C.: The Brookings Institution, 1938), p. 398. See also W. Feuerlein and E. Hannan, *Dollars in Latin America* (New York: Council on Foreign Relations, 1941), chap. 2.

7. J. Guttentag and R. Herring, *The Lender of Last Resort Function in an International Context,* International Finance Section, Princeton University, no. 151, May 1983.

Chapter 2 Appendix

1. J. Cuddington, *Capital Flight: Estimates, Issues and Explanations,* Princeton Studies in International Finance, no. 58, December 1986.

2. R. Dornbusch, "External Debt, Budget Deficits, and Disequilibrium Exchange Rates," in *International Debt and the Developing Countries*, ed. G. Smith and J. Cuddington (Washington, D.C.: World Bank, 1985).

Chapter 3

1. This section draws on R. Dornbusch, "Policy and Performance Links between LDC Debtors and Industrial Countries," *Brookings Papers on Economic Activity* 2 (1985); R. Dornbusch, "Impact on Debtor Countries of World Economic Conditions," in *External Debt, Investment and Growth in Latin America* (Washington, D.C.: International Monetary Fund, 1986); and R. Dornbusch, "International Debt and Economic Instability," in *Debt, Financial Stability and Public Policy* (Reserve Bank of Kansas, 1986).

2. The fact that it is often food subsidies that are eliminated, without the proverbial neutral lump-sum tax to compensate the losers, does not seem to limit the case for the policy recommendation.

3. R. Dornbusch and S. Fischer, "Stopping Hyperinflation: Past and Present," *Weltwirtschaftliches Archiv* (April 1986); S. Fischer, "Sharing the Burden of the International Debt Crisis," *American Economic Review*, Papers and Proceedings (May 1986); and S. Fischer, "Issues in Medium-Term Adjustment," *Research Observer*, no. 2, World Bank (1986).

4. Since the return to voluntary lending was dependent on a restoration of the debtor countries' credit standing, the problems are complicated by confusion about exactly what is meant by "creditworthiness." Originally it meant a reduction of ratios of debt to GDP and debt to exports. It is apparent from the table below that by these measures creditworthiness has deteriorated since 1982.

Creditworthiness (Percent)

	Debt/GDP			Debt/Exports		
	1978	1982	1988	1978	1982	1988
Problem Debtors	31.3	43.6	50.3	179.1	241.1	284.9
Baker 15	29.9	42.3	47.2	203.4	267.8	308.3
Latin America	31.8	43.6	44.8	217.2	271.4	309.5

Source: International Monetary Fund, *World Economic Outlook*, April 1986 and October 1988.

Chapter 4

1. See Bank for International Settlements, *International Banking and Financial Markets Development* (October 1986).

Chapter 5

1. M. Friedman, *Politics and Tyranny* (San Francisco: Pacific Institute for Public Policy Research, 1984); A. Meltzer, "The International Debt Problem," *The Cato Journal* (Spring/Summer 1984); and A. Meltzer, ed., *International Lending and the IMF* (Washington, D.C.: Heritage Foundation, 1984).

2. P. Kenen, "A Bailout for the Banks," *The New York Times,* March 6, 1983; and "Outline of a Proposal for an International Debt Discount Corporation," unpublished manuscript, Princeton University, May 1983.

3. W. Bradley, "A Proposal for Third World Debt Management," speech presented in Zurich, June 29, 1986, and "Defusing the Latin American Debt Bomb," *Washington Post,* October 5, 1986; D. Obey and P. S. Sarbanes, "Recycling Surpluses to the Third World," *The New York Times,* November 9, 1986; C. Schumer, "The Schumer Option Plan for Third World Debt Relief," unpublished manuscript, 1987; F. Rohatyn, "The State of the Banks," *The New York Review of Books,* November 4, 1982, and "A Plan for Stretching Out Global Debt," *Business Week,* February 28, 1983; H. Kaufman, "Debt in a Difficult-to-Control Financial System," talk delivered before the Congressional Summit on Debt and Trade, New York, December 1986; "The Risks in the World Economic Order," public lecture, New York University, February 24, 1987; R. Weinert, "Banks and Bankruptcy," *Foreign Policy* (Spring 1983), and "Swapping Third-World Debt," *Foreign Policy* (Winter 1986-87); and B. Cohen, "Third World Debt," *The New York Times*, March 5, 1987.

4. See Morgan Guaranty, "LDC Debt Realities," *World Financial Markets,* (June/July 1986).

5. The standard restructuring program with new money is organized so that it is difficult for banks to take out the money the IMF puts in. The IMF recognized this temptation in the Turkish stabilization program in the late 1970s and in 1981 pointed out that there was a need to maintain bank involvement in the lending process. See B. Nowzad and R. Williams, *External Indebtedness of Developing Countries* (Washington, D.C.: International Monetary Fund, May 1981).

6. For estimates on the magnitude of capital flight see Morgan Guaranty, *World Financial Markets*, March 1986; J. Cuddington, *Capital Flight: Estimates, Issues and Explanations*, Princeton Studies in International Finance, no. 58, December 1986; and M. Watson et al., *International Capital Markets* (Washington, D.C.: International Monetary Fund, December 1986). Recent surveys include D. Lessard and J. Williamson, *Financial Intermediation Beyond the Debt Crisis* (Washington, D.C.: Institute for International Econom-

ics, 1985); and M. Doppler and M. Williamson, "Capital Flight: Concepts, Measurement and Issues," *Staff Studies for the World Economic Outlook* (Washington, D.C.: International Monetary Fund, August 1987).

7. The Turkish experience is documented in D. Rodrik, "External Debt and Economic Performance," unpublished manuscript, John F. Kennedy School of Government, Harvard University, 1986.

8. The Turkish deposit facility is different from the Mex-dollar scheme, where within the country foreign currency deposits are allowed. In the Mexican case, much of the demand comes from a shift out of a home currency deposit, though perhaps it also serves to dampen or stop capital outflow. In Turkey, the purpose is to acquire command over assets already located abroad. The difference is brought out by the fact that Turkish foreign currency deposits and Dresdener deposits carry quite different interest rates. These differences reflect different jurisdictions, guarantees, and capital mobility and the availability of alternative assets.

9. For a strong statement of support for debt-equity swaps see Morgan Guaranty, *World Financial Markets*, September 1986. See also Watson et al., *International Capital Markets*, and Weinert, "Swapping Third-World Debt."

Chapter 6

1. J. Williamson, "The Outlook for Debt Relief or Repudiation in Latin America," *Oxford Review of Economic Policy* 2, no. 1 (1986), pp. 1-2, has provided some definitions that usefully characterize different events: "A debt *moratorium* occurs when a country declares that it will not pay debt service for a specific period of time. . . . A debt *rescheduling* involves creditors and debtors agreeing to modify the original terms of the loan, typically by extending maturities. . . . Debt *relief* involves modification in the original terms of the loan that reduces the present value of the debtor's obligations. A country *repudiates* its debt when it declares that it does not recognize any responsibility for continuing to pay debt service."

2. A. Meltzer, "International Debt Problems," unpublished manuscript, Carnegie-Mellon University, July 1986, pp. 9-10.

3. M. Friedman, *Politics and Tyranny* (San Francisco: Pacific Institute for Public Policy Research, 1984), p. 38.

4. The agreements between debtor countries and the Bond Holders' Protective Council in the interwar period and through the 1950s gives an idea of what the free market solution might resemble. The typical agreement involved paying 10 percent of arrears and a rescheduling of the full principal at a low interest rate for a twenty- to thirty-year period. Some countries, for example, Mexico, held out much longer than others and settled on terms far less advantageous to the creditors.

5. A. Meltzer, "The International Debt Problem," *The Cato Journal*

(Spring/Summer 1984); and A. Meltzer, ed., *International Lending and the IMF* (Washington, D.C.: Heritage Foundation, 1984).

6. From the preface to the 1961 *Annual Report* of the Foreign Bond Holders' Protective Council, which was set up to help individuals collect private debts from foreign countries.

7. S. Fischer, "Sharing the Burden of the International Debt Crisis," *American Economic Review*, Papers and Proceedings (May 1986); S. Fischer, "Issues in Medium-Term Adjustment," *Research Observer*, no. 2, World Bank (1986); and J. Sachs, "Managing the LDC Debt Crisis," *Brookings Papers on Economic Activity* 2 (1986), discuss the domestic legal practice on the rewriting of contracts.

8. J.M. Keynes, *A Tract on Monetary Reform* (New York: St. Martin's Press, 1971), pp. 56-57.

9. See H. Breck, "African Relief, Spelled D-E-F-A-U-L-T," *The Wall Street Journal*, November 7, 1986, for a recommendation that some African countries should default. Professor Jeffrey Sachs of Harvard University has recommended default in the case of Bolivia.

Chapter 7

1. For an exposition of this view, see P. Bauer, "Ethics and Etiquette of Third World Debt," *Ethics and International Affairs* 1 (1987).

2. U.S. Congress, Subcommittee on International Development, Institutions and Finance, House Committee on Banking, Finance and Urban Affairs, *Hearings on the Third World Debt,* March 3, 1987.

3. See James Baker III, testimony before the Senate Committee on Governmental Affairs, March 25, 1987. Identical wording was used in a speech by Deputy Secretary of State John Whitehead on April 6, 1987.

4. Address before the Presidential Leadership Summit on Debt, Trade and the Dollar, Washington, D.C., September 19, 1988.

5. R. Bench, statement before the Senate Committee on Banking, Housing, and Urban Affairs, Subcommittee on International Finance, April 2, 1987; and C. Schumer, "The Schumer Option Plan for Third World Debt Relief," unpublished manuscript, 1987, for a very comparable suggestion that different banks need choices on the best way of participating in the debt restructuring process.

Chapter 8

1. See testimony by Robert Bench, deputy controller of the currency, before the Senate Committee on Banking, Housing and Monetary Policy, April 2, 1987.

2. Such a proposal was presented by Franz Luthof, the president of a major Swiss bank, at the December 1986 Congressional Summit on Trade and Debt in New York and in the *Neue Zurcher Zeitung.*

3. P. Kenen, "A Bailout for the Banks," *The New York Times*, March 6, 1983, and "Outline of a Proposal for an International Debt Discount Corporation," unpublished manuscript, Princeton University, May 1983.

4. R. Weinert, "Swapping Third-World Debt," *Foreign Policy* (Winter 1986–87).

5. H. Kaufman, "Debt in a Difficult-to-Control Financial System," talk delivered before the Congressional Summit on Debt and Trade, New York, December 1986.

6. James Robinson III, "A Comprehensive Agenda for LDC Debt and World Trade Growth," *The AMEX Bank Review*, no. 13, March 1988.

7. See the report in the *Financial Times,* May 21, 1987.

8. For a recent evaluation of market-based debt reduction schemes, see J. Bulow and K. Rogoff, "The Debt Buy-Back Boondoggle," *Brookings Papers on Economic Activity* 2, 1988, and the discussants' comments; P. J. Krugman, "Market-Based Debt Reduction Schemes," NBER Working Paper, 1987; M. Corden, "An International Debt Facility," IMF *Staff Papers*, September 1988; J. Williamson, *Voluntary Approaches to Debt Reduction*, Institute for International Economics, 1988; and K. Froot, "Debt Buy-Backs," mimeo, Massachusetts Institute of Technology, 1988.

Chapter 9

1. Remarks by Secretary of the Treasury James A. Baker III to the Bretton Woods Committee Annual Meeting, Washington, D.C., February 16, 1988.

2. The most complete study of the scope for sanctions is A. Kaletsky, *The Costs of Default* (New York: Priority Press Publications, 1985). Kaletsky concludes that sanctions should not be an overriding concern in the case of Brazil.

3. J. Kraft, *The Mexican Rescue* (New York: Group of Thirty, 1984).

Index